P9-CAA-038

California Science

PEARSON
Scott Foresman

Editorial Offices: Glenview, Illinois • Parsippany, New Jersey • New York, New York
Sales Offices: Boston, Massachusetts • Duluth, Georgia • Glenview, Illinois • Coppell, Texas • Sacramento, California • Mesa, Arizona

Series Authors

Dr. Timothy Cooney
Professor of Earth Science and Science Education
University of Northern Iowa (UNI)
Cedar Falls, Iowa

Dr. Jim Cummins
Professor
Department of Curriculum, Teaching, and Learning
University of Toronto
Toronto, Canada

Dr. James Flood
Distinguished Professor of Literacy and Language
School of Teacher Education
San Diego State University
San Diego, California

Barbara Kay Foots, M.Ed.
Science Education Consultant
Houston, Texas

Dr. M. Jenice Goldston
Associate Professor of Science Education
Department of Elementary Education Programs
University of Alabama
Tuscaloosa, Alabama

Dr. Shirley Gholston Key
Associate Professor of Science Education
Instruction and Curriculum Leadership Department
College of Education
University of Memphis
Memphis, Tennessee

Dr. Diane Lapp
Distinguished Professor of Reading and Language Arts in Teacher Education
San Diego State University
San Diego, California

Sheryl A. Mercier
Classroom Teacher
Dunlap Elementary School
Dunlap, California

Karen L. Ostlund
UTeach Specialist
College of Natural Sciences
The University of Texas at Austin
Austin, Texas

Dr. Nancy Romance
Professor of Science Education & Principal Investigator
NSF/IERI Science IDEAS Project
Charles E. Schmidt College of Science
Florida Atlantic University
Boca Raton, Florida

Dr. William Tate
Chair and Professor of Education and Applied Statistics
Department of Education
Washington University
St. Louis, Missouri

Dr. Kathryn C. Thornton
Former NASA Astronaut
Professor
School of Engineering and Applied Science
University of Virginia
Charlottesville, Virginia

Dr. Leon Ukens
Professor Emeritus
Department of Physics, Astronomy, and Geosciences
Towson University
Towson, Maryland

Steve Weinberg
Consultant
Connecticut Center for Advanced Technology
East Hartford, Connecticut

ISBN: 0-328-18837-9

6 7 8 9 10 V082 15 14 13 12 11 10 09 08

Contributing Author

Dr. Michael P. Klentschy
Superintendent
El Centro Elementary School District
El Centro, California

Consulting Author

Dr. Olga Amaral
Chair, Division of Teacher Education
San Diego State University
Calexico, California

Science Content Consultants

Dr. Herbert Brunkhorst
Chair
Department of Science, Mathematics and Technology
College of Education
California State University, San Bernardino
San Bernardino, California

Dr. Karen Kolehmainen
Department of Physics
California State University, San Bernardino
San Bernardino, California

Dr. Stephen D. Lewis
Earth and Environmental Sciences
California State University, Fresno
Fresno, California

 Content Consultants

Adena Williams Loston, Ph.D.
Chief Education Officer
Office of the Chief Education Officer

Clifford W. Houston, Ph.D.
Deputy Chief Education Officer for Education Programs
Office of the Chief Education Officer

Frank C. Owens
Senior Policy Advisor
Office of the Chief Education Officer

Deborah Brown Biggs
Manager, Education Flight Projects Office
Space Operations Mission Directorate, Education Lead

Erika G. Vick
NASA Liaison to Pearson Scott Foresman
Education Flight Projects Office

William E. Anderson
Partnership Manager for Education
Aeronautics Research Mission Directorate

Anita Krishnamurthi
Program Planning Specialist
Space Science Education and Outreach Program

Bonnie J. McClain
Chief of Education
Exploration Systems Mission Directorate

Diane Clayton, Ph.D.
Program Scientist
Earth Science Education

Deborah Rivera
Strategic Alliances Manager
Office of Public Affairs
NASA Headquarters

Douglas D. Peterson
Public Affairs Office, Astronaut Office
Office of Public Affairs
NASA Johnson Space Center

Nicole Cloutier
Public Affairs Office, Astronaut Office
Office of Public Affairs
NASA Johnson Space Center

Reviewers

Elaine Chasse-DeMers
Teacher
Taylor Street School
Sacramento, California

Kevin Clevenger
Teacher
Oak Chan Elementary
Folsom, California

Kim Eddings
Teacher
Madison Elementary
Pomona, California

Joseph Frescatore
Teacher
Chavez Elementary
San Diego, California

Candace Gibbons
Teacher
Freedom Elementary
Clovis, California

Anne Higginbotham
Teacher
Arundel Elementary
San Carlos, California

Sean Higgins
Teacher
Monte Verde Elementary
San Bruno, California

Sharon Janulaw
Science Education Specialist
Sonoma County Office of Education
Santa Rosa, California

Jeanne E. Martin
Teacher
John Gill School
Redwood City, California

Mark Allen Schultz
Teacher
Theodore Judah Elementary
Folsom, California

Corinne Schwartz
Teacher
Lincrest Elementary
Yuba City, California

Schelly T. Solko
Teacher
Loudon School
Bakersfield, California

Bobbie Stumbaugh
Teacher
Roy Cloud School
Redwood City, California

Kimberly Thiesen
Teacher
Freedom Elementary
Clovis, California

Carole Bialek Vargas
Teacher
Empire Oaks Elementary
Folsom, California

Bonita J. Walker-Davis
Teacher
Don Riggio School
Stockton, California

Debra Willsie
Teacher
Tarpey Elementary
Clovis, California

Olivia Winslow
Teacher
Earl Warren Elementary
Sacramento, California

California Science

How can things be described?

Chapter 1 • Observing Solids, Liquids, and Gases

Chapter 2 • Changing Solids, Liquids, and Gases

How can things be changed?

CALIFORNIA Unit B Life Sciences

What do plants and animals need?

Chapter 3 • Needs of Plants and Animals

Where do plants and animals live?

Chapter 4 • Environments

Chapter 5 • Plants and Animals Living Together

How do plants and animals live together?

How can you tell about the weather?

Chapter 6 • Observing Weather

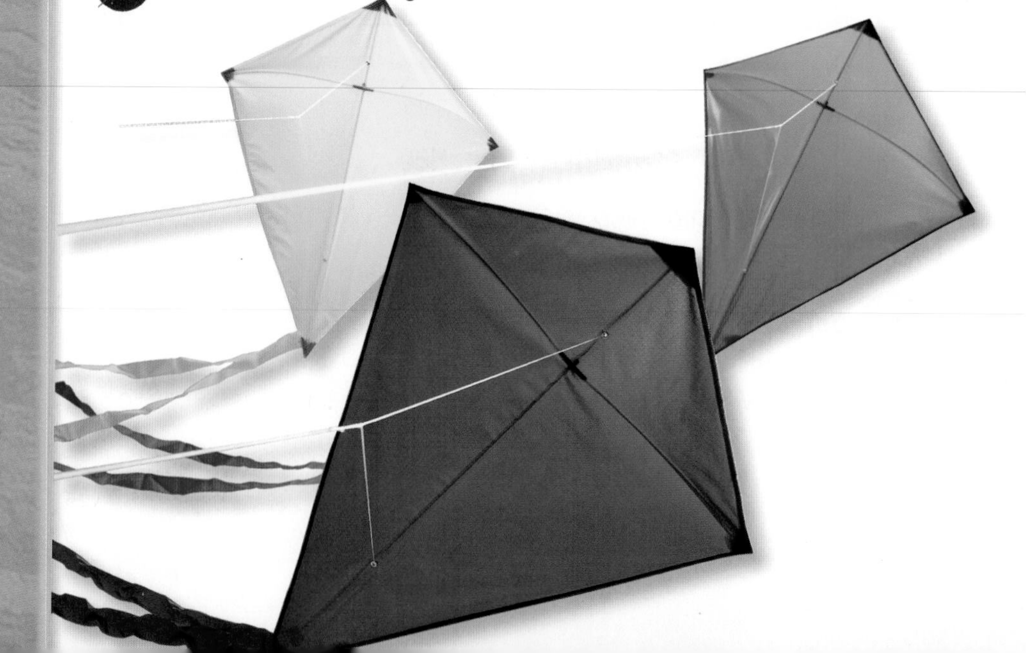

Chapter 7 • Seasons

What is the weather like in different seasons?

Science Process Skills

Observe

A scientist who wants to find out about the ocean observes many things. You use your senses to find out about things too.

Classify

Scientists classify living things in the ocean. You classify when you sort or group things by their properties.

Estimate and Measure

Scientists can estimate the size of living things in the ocean. This means they make a careful guess about the size or amount of something. Then they measure it.

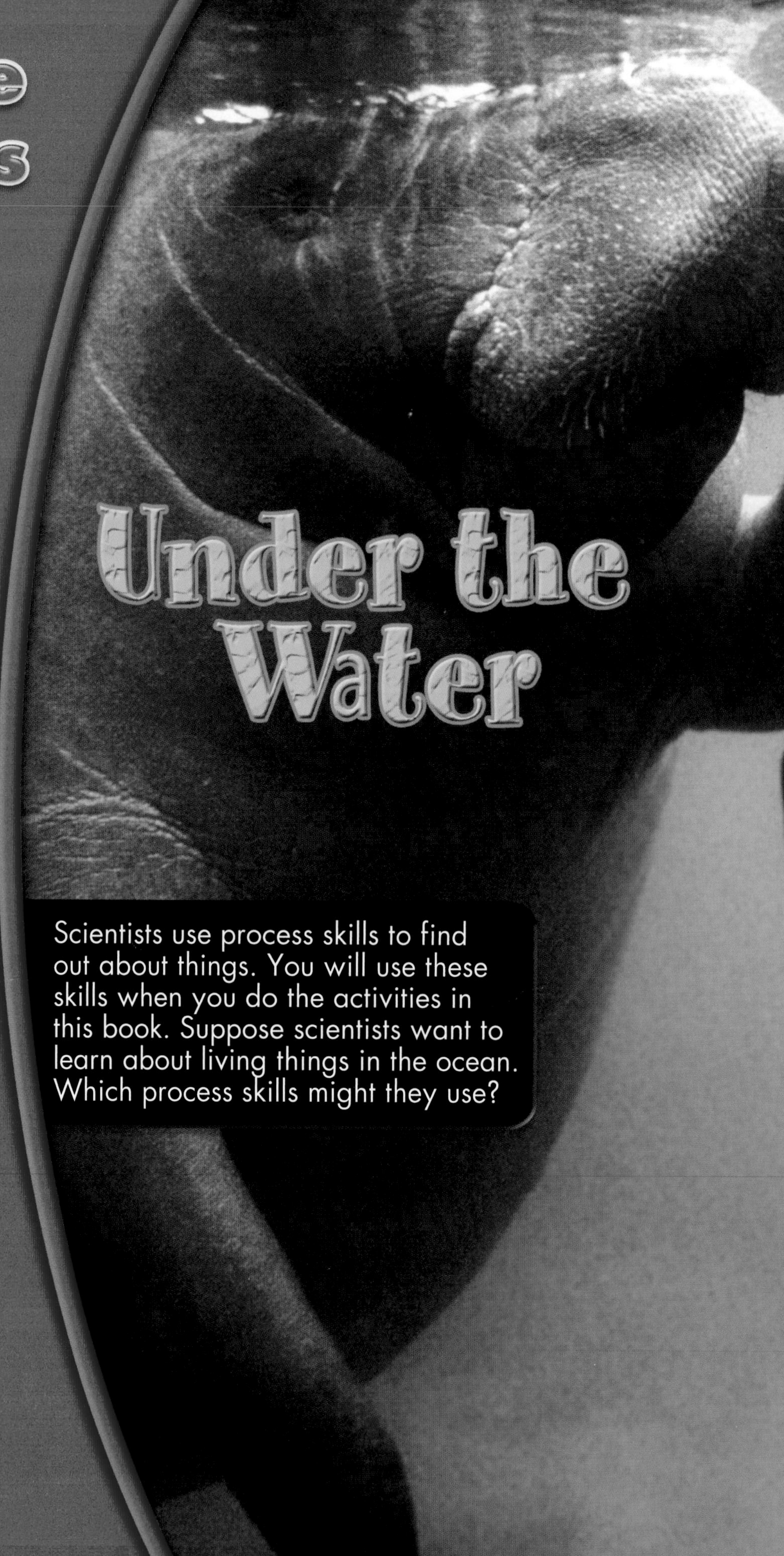

Under the Water

Scientists use process skills to find out about things. You will use these skills when you do the activities in this book. Suppose scientists want to learn about living things in the ocean. Which process skills might they use?

Infer

Scientists are always learning about living things in the ocean. Scientists draw a conclusion or make a guess from what they already know.

Predict

Scientists tell what they think they will find before they go into the ocean.

Make and Use Models

Scientists might make and use models. Models show what they already know.

Science Process Skills

Investigate and Experiment

Scientists plan and do an investigation as they study the ocean.

Make Hypotheses

Think of a question you have about living things in the ocean. Make a statement that you can test to answer your question.

Control Variables

Scientists plan a fair test. Scientists change only one thing in their test. Scientists keep everything else the same.

Collect Data

Scientists record what they observe and measure. Scientists put this data into charts or graphs.

Suppose you were a scientist. You might want to learn more about the ocean. What questions might you have? How would you use process skills to help you learn?

Interpret Data

Scientists use what they learn to solve problems or answer questions.

Communicate

Scientists tell what they learn about living things in the ocean.

Lab zone

Using Scientific Methods for Science Inquiry

Scientific methods are ways of finding answers. Scientific methods have these steps. Sometimes scientists do the steps in a different order. Scientists do not always do all of the steps.

Ask a question.

Ask a question that you want answered.

Do seeds need water to grow?

Make a hypothesis.

Tell what you think the answer is to your question.

If seeds are watered, then they will grow.

Plan a fair test.

Change only one thing.

Keep everything else the same.

Water one pot with seeds.

no water

water

Do your test.

Test your hypothesis. Do your test more than once. See if your results are the same.

Record what happens.

Keep records of what you find out. Use words or drawings to help.

Tell your conclusions.

Observe the results of your test. Decide if your hypothesis is right or wrong. Tell what you decide.

Seeds need water to grow.

no water

water

Go further.

Use what you learn. Think of new questions or better ways to do a test.

- Ask a Question
- Make a Hypothesis
- Plan a Fair Test
- Do Your Test
- Record What Happens
- Tell Your Conclusions
- Go Further

Wind vane
You can use a wind vane to tell which direction the wind is blowing. A wind vane points into the wind.

Scientists use many different kinds of tools.

Safety goggles
You can use safety goggles to protect your eyes.

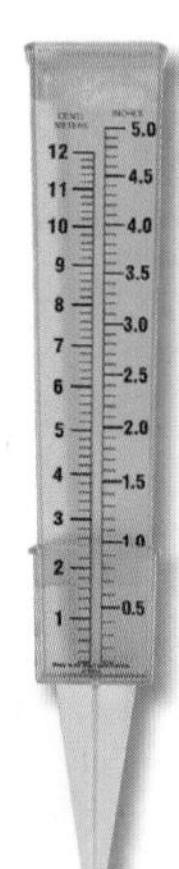

Rain gauge
You can use a rain gauge to measure how much rain falls.

Meterstick
You can use a meterstick to measure how long something is. Scientists use a meterstick to measure in meters.

Metric ruler
You can use a metric ruler to measure how long something is. Scientists use a metric ruler to measure in centimeters and millimeters.

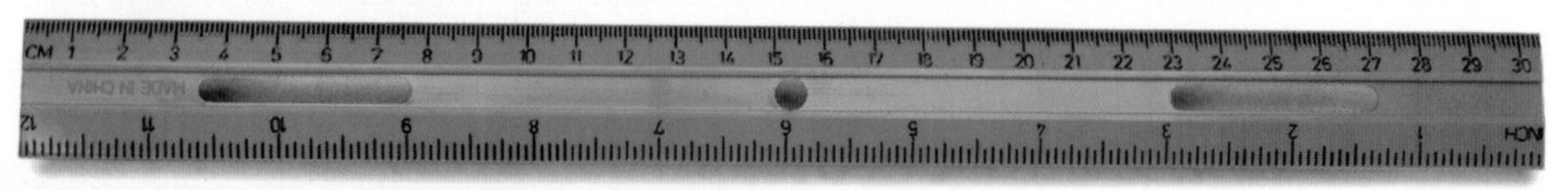

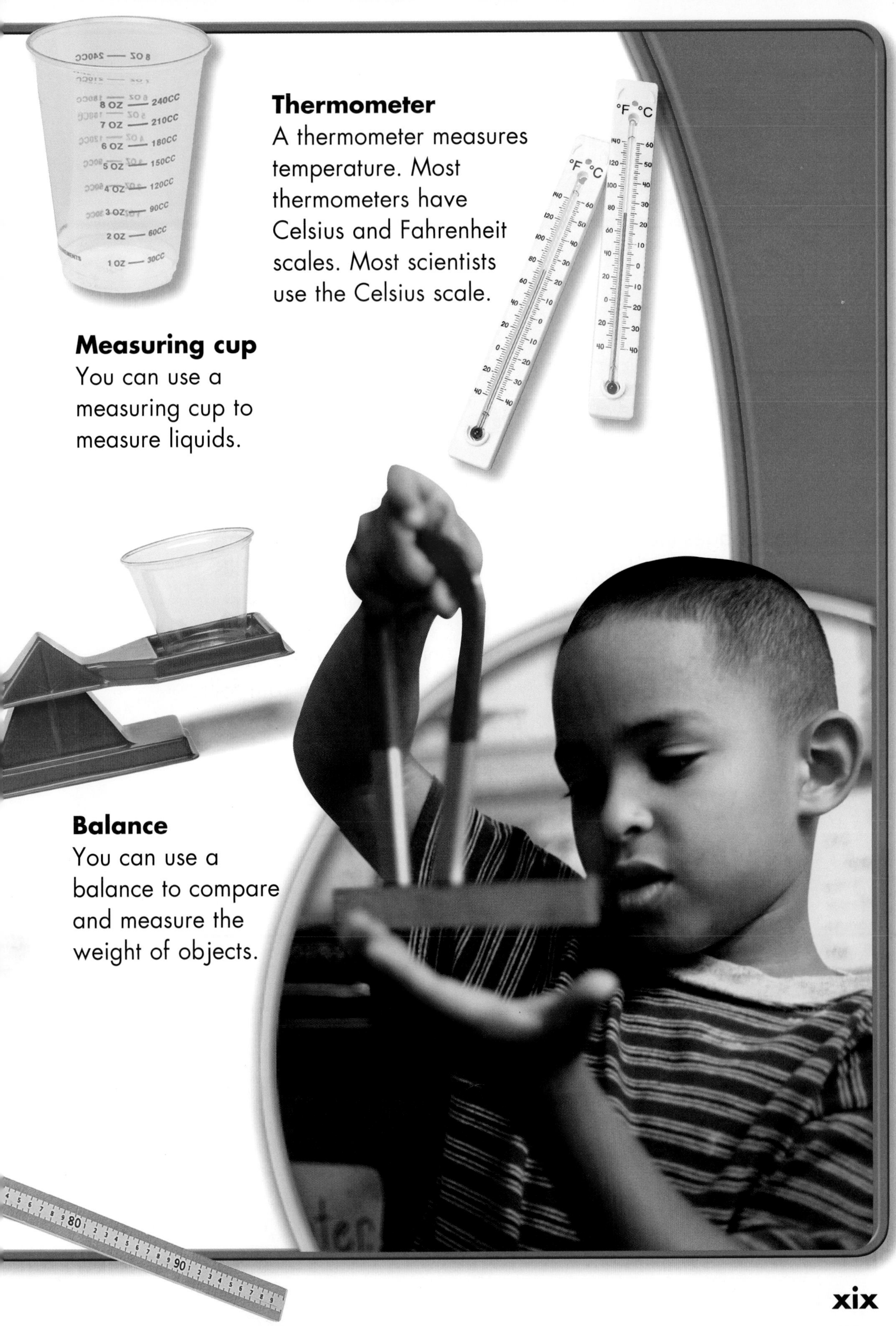

Thermometer
A thermometer measures temperature. Most thermometers have Celsius and Fahrenheit scales. Most scientists use the Celsius scale.

Measuring cup
You can use a measuring cup to measure liquids.

Balance
You can use a balance to compare and measure the weight of objects.

Safety in the Classroom

You need to be careful when doing science activities. These pages include safety tips to remember:

- Listen to your teacher.
- Read each activity carefully.
- Never taste or smell materials unless your teacher tells you to.
- Wear safety goggles when needed.
- Handle scissors and other equipment carefully.
- Keep your work place neat and clean.
- Clean up spills right away.

- Tell your teacher about accidents.
- Tell your teacher if you see something that looks unsafe.
- Put things away when you finish an activity.
- Return all materials to their proper places.
- Throw all trash in the trash can.
- Wash your hands well after every activity.

Safety at Home

Safety Tips

- Put toys, shoes, and books away. Do not leave anything lying on the floor.
- Do not play with sharp objects such as knives.
- Wash your hands with soap and warm water before eating.
- Clean up all spills right away.
- Do not run indoors or jump down stairs.

Fire Safety Tips

- Never use matches or lighters.
- Never use the stove or oven without the help of an adult.
- Get out quickly if your home is on fire.
- Stop, drop, and roll if your clothing catches on fire. Do not run.
- Know two ways to get out of your home.
- Practice fire escape routes with your family.

Electrical Safety Tips

- Do not touch electrical outlets.
- Use the plug to pull out an electrical cord. Do not pull the cord.
- Keep all electrical objects away from water.

Earthquake Tips

- Make a plan with an adult about what to do if there is an earthquake.
- Get under or lie next to a heavy table, desk, or piece of furniture.
- Stay away from glass doors and windows.
- Help your family make an earthquake kit. Put water, food, a flashlight, and a radio in your kit.

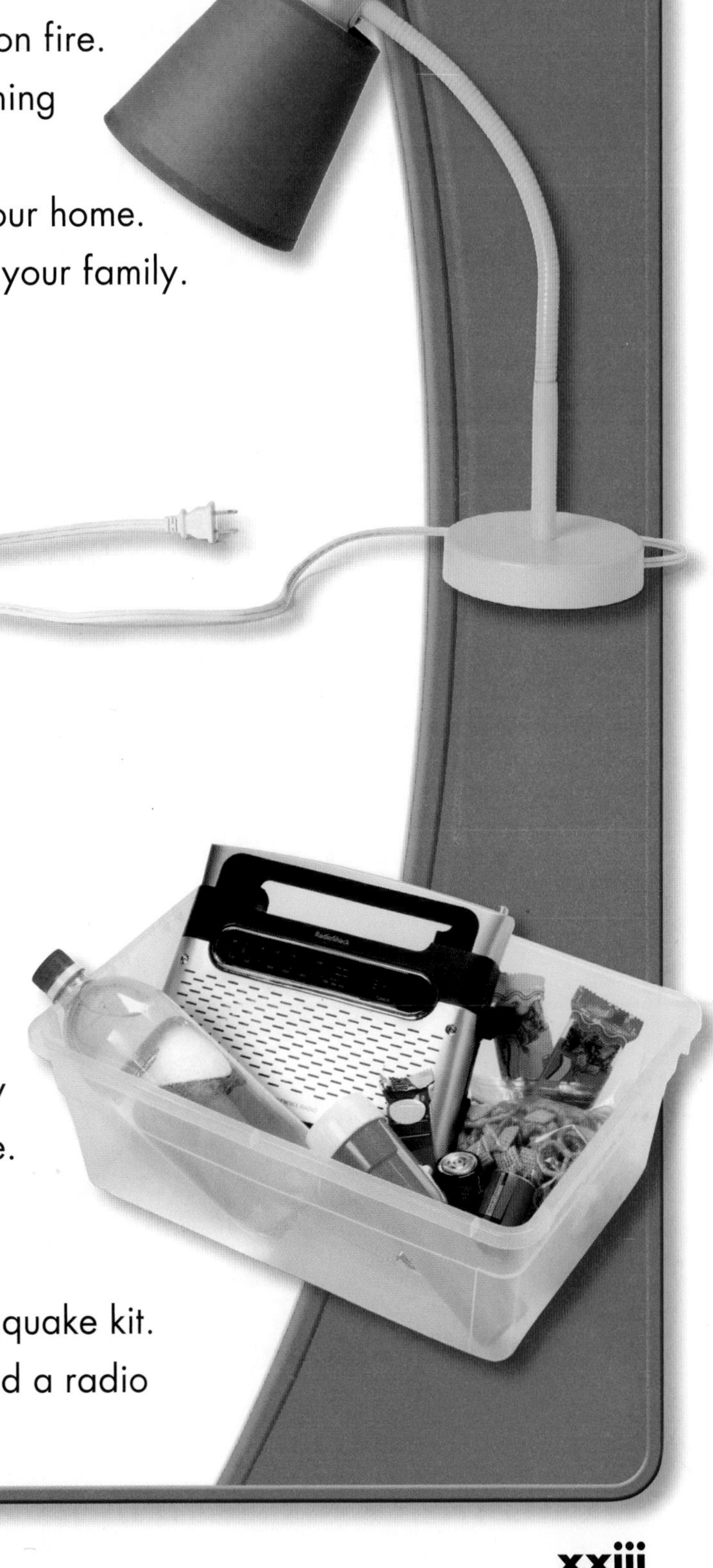

Metric and Customary Measurement

Science uses the metric system to measure things. Metric measurement is used around the world. Here is how different metric measurements compare to customary measurement.

Length and Distance

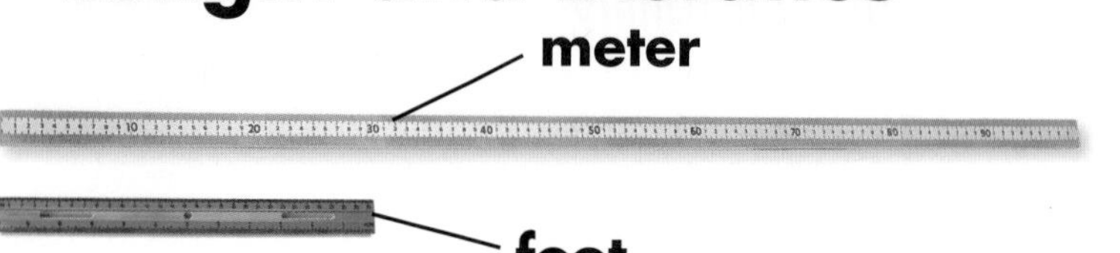

One meter is longer than 3 feet.

Liquid Volume

One liter is greater than 4 cups.

Weight and Mass

One kilogram is greater than one pound.

Temperature

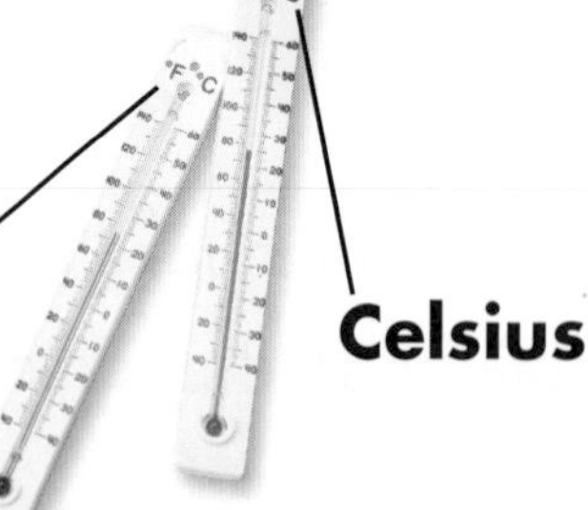

Water freezes at 0°C and 32°F.

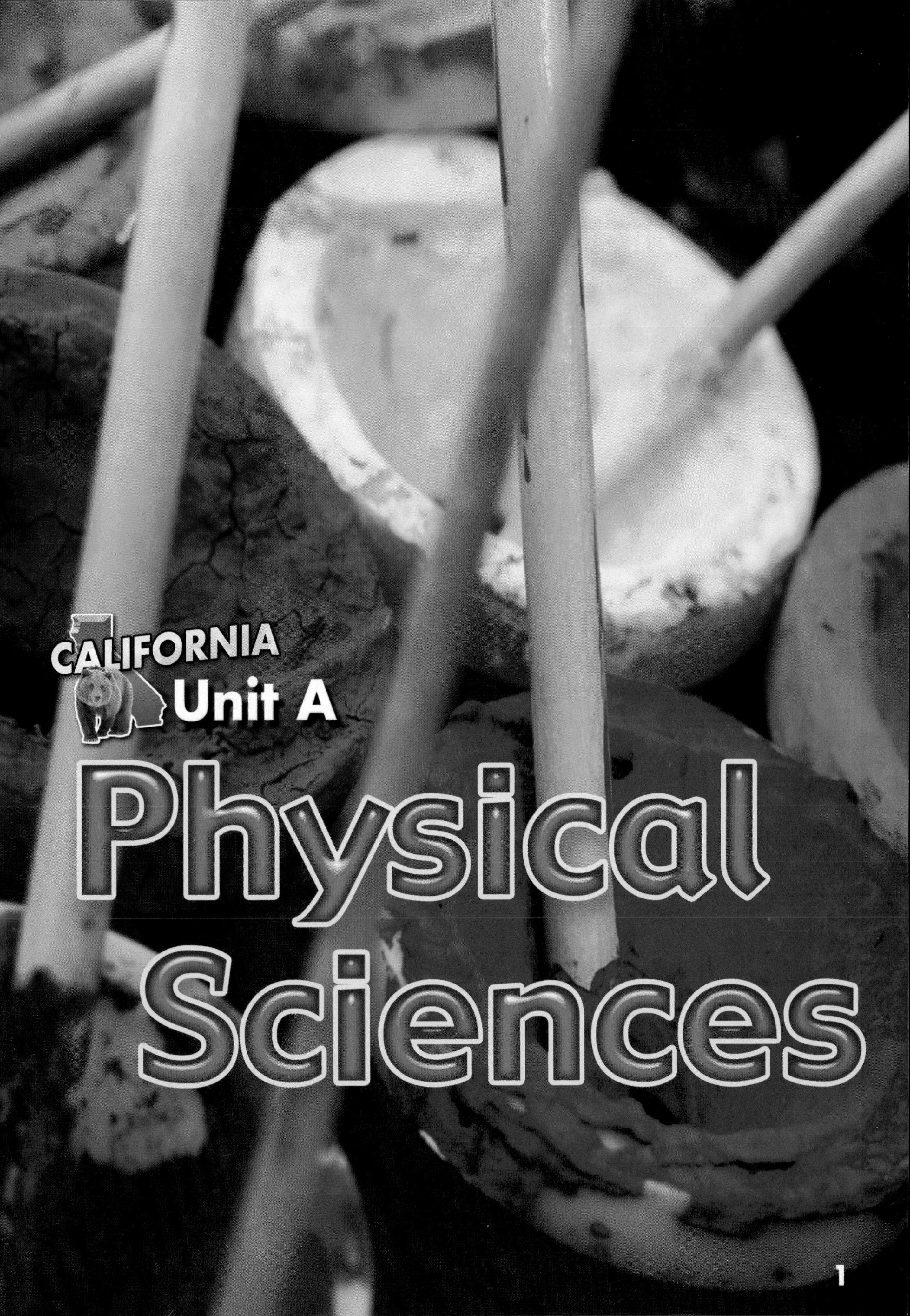

CALIFORNIA

Unit A

Physical Sciences

California Field Trip

Ocean Beach Kite Festival

San Diego, California

The Ocean Beach Kite Festival is in San Diego. You can learn to make and fly a kite. You can march in a parade down to the beach.

Find out more.

Research to find out more about kites.

- Draw a picture of a kite you would like to make. Tell how big the kite will be. Tell about the shape of the kite.

San Diego

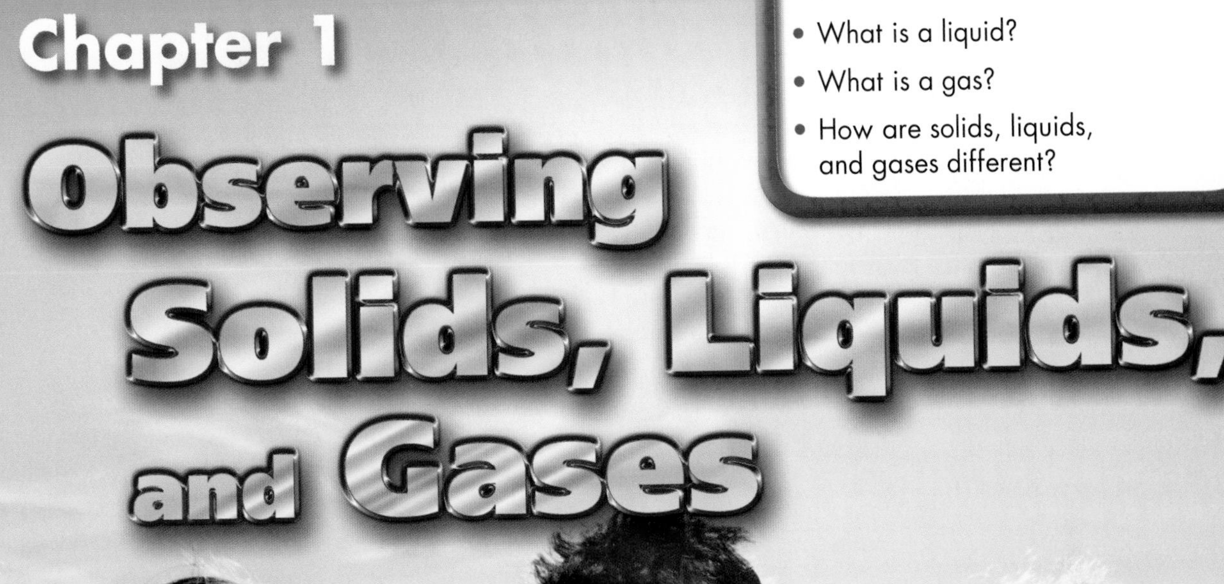

CALIFORNIA Standards Focus Questions

- What is a property?
- What is a solid?
- What is a liquid?
- What is a gas?
- How are solids, liquids, and gases different?

Chapter 1

Observing Solids, Liquids, and Gases

Focus on the BIG Idea

How can things be described?

DIGITAL

Chapter 1 Vocabulary

property page 9

solid page 12

liquid page 16

gas page 18

property

liquid

gas

Lab zone Directed Inquiry

Explore What can change shape?

Materials

bag with colored water

wooden block

What to Do

1. Touch the bag. **Observe.**

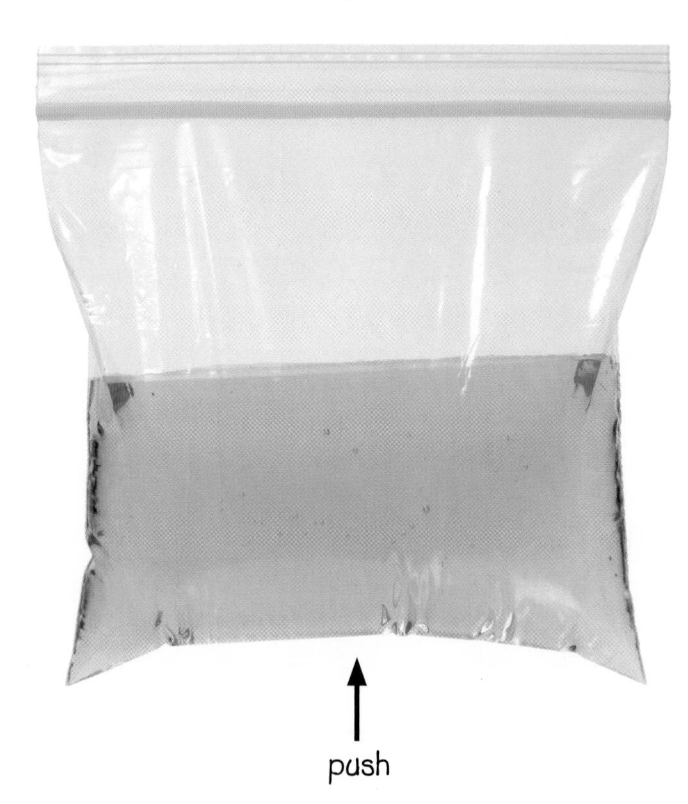

2. Touch the block. Observe.

push

3. Compare. Record.

Explain Your Results

Which changed shape?
Which kept its shape?

Process Skills

You can touch an object to make an **observation.**

How to Read Science

Reading Skills

Use Context Clues

Pictures can give you clues about what you read.

Science Story

Building Blocks

Blocks are different sizes. Blocks are different shapes. Building with blocks is fun!

Apply It!

Observe How are the blocks different? Look for clues in the picture.

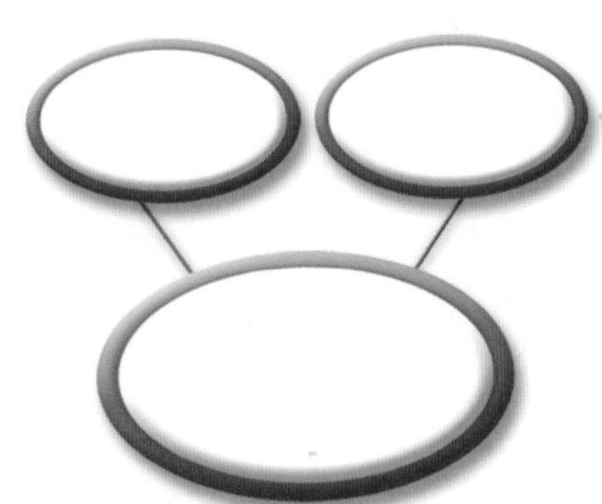

You Are There

Making Bubbles

Sung to the tune of "I've Been Working on the Railroad"
Lyrics by Gerri Brioso & Richard Freitas/The Dovetail Group, Inc.

The bubble wand is something solid,
With one end that is round.
The bubble wand is big and yellow.
It feels smooth is what I found.

Lesson 1

What is a property?

Swoosh! Look at the bubble.
The bubble has properties.
A **property** is something that you can observe with your senses.

Size is a property.
Is the bubble big or small?

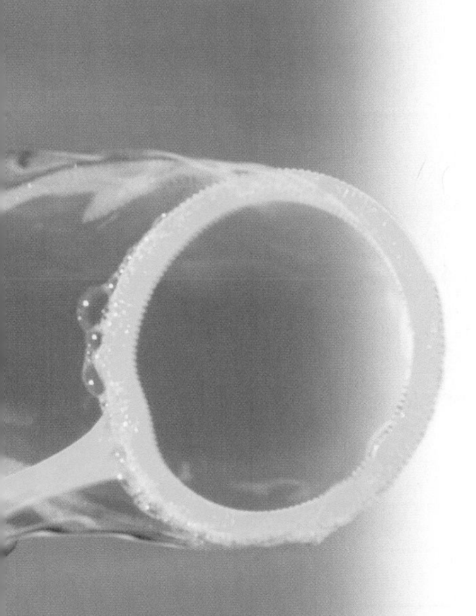

What words can you use to tell about the bubble?

Properties of Objects

Look at the objects in the picture. What colors do you see? What shapes do you see?

Color and shape are properties. How something feels is a property too.

The shape of the door is a rectangle. The door feels hard.

1. What is a property?
2. Make a chart like this one. Fill it in with words that tell about each thing.

	Color	Feel
door		
basket		
boots		

The scarf
feels soft.
What shape is
the cloth bag?
What shape is
the green ball?
The red boots
feel smooth.
The brown basket
feels bumpy.

Lesson 2

What is a solid?

Some things are solids.
A **solid** has its
own shape.
A solid has its
own size too.

These toys are solids.

Look at the blocks. What shapes do you see?

A solid does not change shape when it is moved from place to place.

1. Checkpoint What is a solid?

TARGET SKILL

2. **Use Context Clues** What are 2 properties of wooden blocks? Look for clues in the picture.

Weight

Weight is a property too.
Weight is how heavy something is.

A balance compares the weights of objects. The object that goes down weighs more.

DIGITAL Look for Active Art animations at www.pearsonsuccessnet.com

Some objects weigh more than other objects.
Look at the toy bear.
Look at the baseball.
Which weighs more?

Lesson Review

1. What is weight?
2. **Writing in Science**
   Describe how heavy your pencil feels.

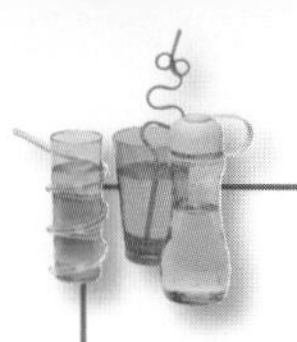

Lesson 3

What is a liquid?

Some things are liquids.

A **liquid** takes the shape of its container.

A liquid has its own amount or size.

You can pour a liquid.

Water is a liquid. What are some other liquids?

Look at these cups.
Each cup has a different shape.
Each cup holds the same amount of liquid.

Measuring cups show the amount or size of liquids.

Lesson Review

1. What is a liquid?
2. **Use Context Clues** How can liquids be different? Look for clues in the pictures.

TARGET SKILL

Lesson 4

What is a gas?

Look at the balloons.
The balloons are filled with air.
Air is a gas.

A **gas** can change shape and size.
A gas takes the size and
shape of its container.
You cannot see most gases.

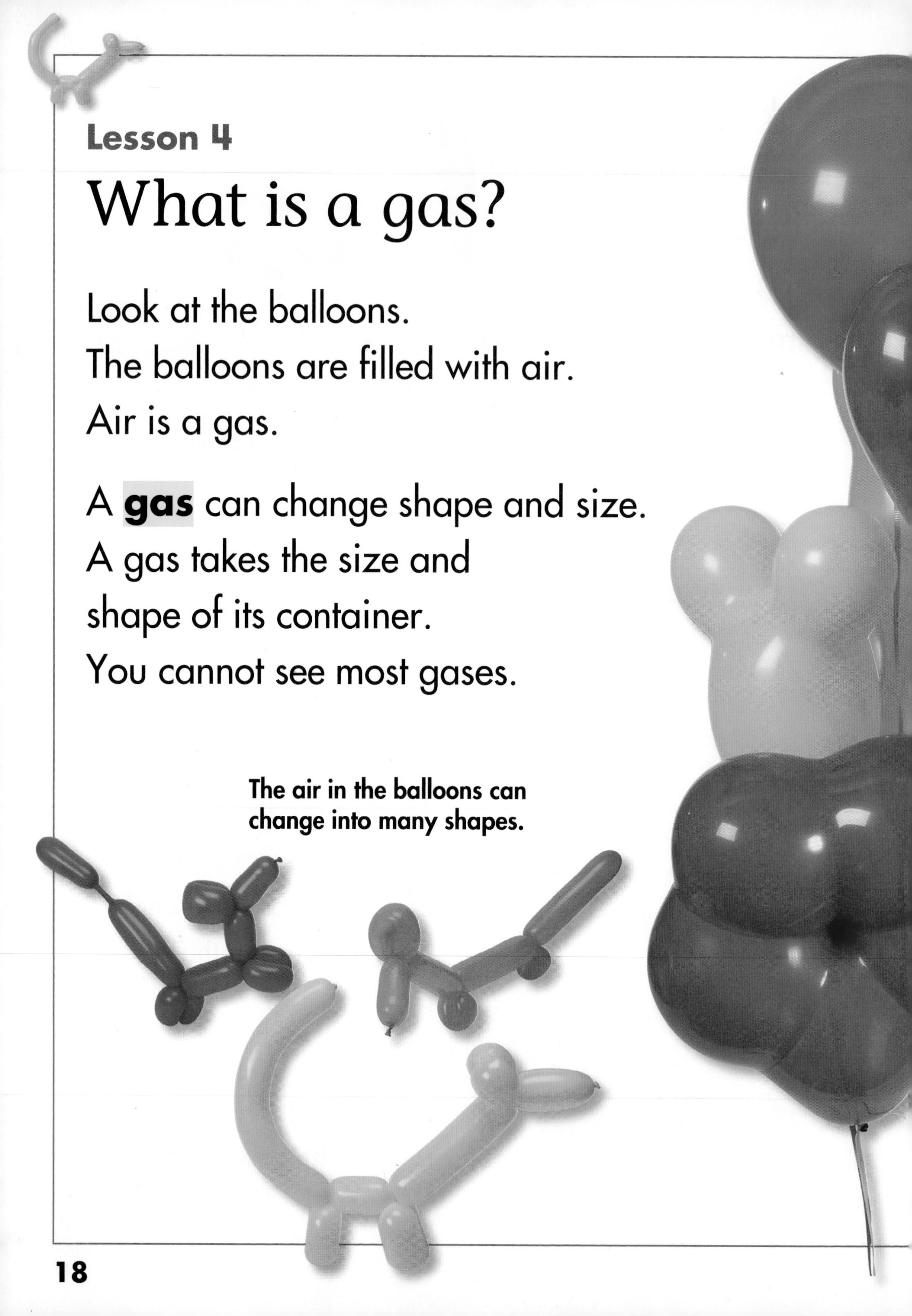

The air in the balloons can change into many shapes.

See how high the water is.

Air takes up space. The air in the balloon pushes the water up.

Lesson Review

1. What is a gas?
2. Writing in Science Write a complete sentence. Can you see most gases?

Lesson 5

How are solids, liquids, and gases different?

Solids, liquids, and gases are different.

A solid has its own shape.
A liquid takes the shape of its container.
A gas takes the shape of its container too.

A solid has its own size.
A liquid has its own amount or size too.
A gas takes the size of its container.

Can you find the solids, liquids, and gases on the table?

✓Lesson Review

1. How is the shape of a solid different from the shape of a liquid or a gas?
2. How is the size of a gas different from the size of a solid or a liquid?

Describing the Position of Objects

You can use an object to describe where other objects are.

This orange block is below and next to the yellow block.

Look at the block tower.
Find the long red block.

1. How many blocks are above the red block?
2. Find the block above and next to the red block. What color is that block?
3. Find a block below and left of the red block. What color is that block?

Lab zone **Take-Home Activity**

Find blocks of different colors, shapes, or sizes. Tell a friend where to place each block to build a tower. Take turns.

Lab zone Guided Inquiry

Investigate How much space does a liquid take up?

Materials

3 measuring cups (one with colored water)

red crayon

What to Do

1. **Observe.** How much water is in the first cup?

2. Pour. How much water is in the next cup? Color in the chart.

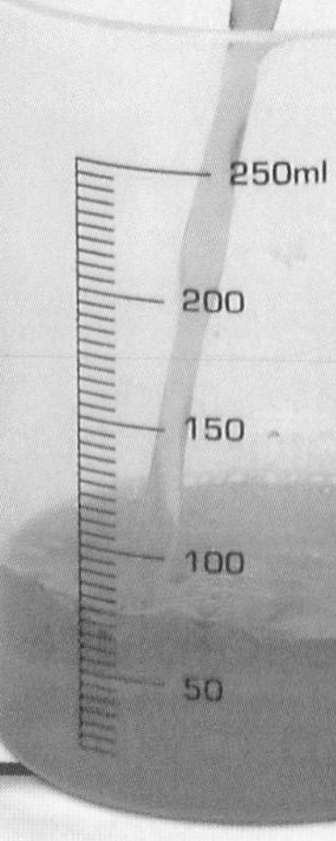

Process Skills

You can **observe** and record with numbers and pictures.

DIGITAL Lab zone

3 Pour. How much water is in the last cup? Color in the chart.

Explain Your Results

1. How much water was in each cup? Record on the chart.
2. **Observe.** How did the shape of the water change?

Go Further

What will happen if you use a different liquid? Find out.

Chapter 1 Reviewing Key Concepts

Focus on the BIG Idea

Shape, size, weight, or feel are ways to describe solids, liquids, and gases.

Lesson 1

What is a property?

- A property is something you can observe with your senses.
- Shape, size, color, and how something feels are properties.

Lesson 2

What is a solid?

- A solid has its own shape and size.

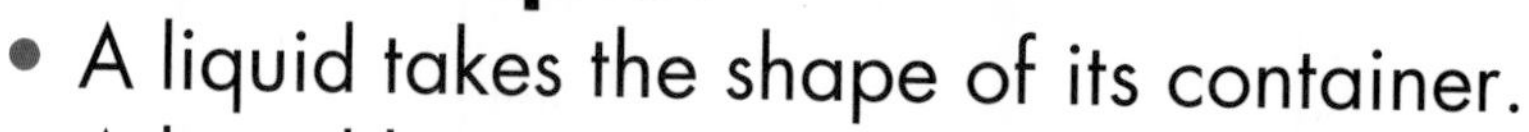

Lesson 3

What is a liquid?

- A liquid takes the shape of its container.
- A liquid has its own amount or size.

Lesson 4

What is a gas?

- Air is a gas.
- A gas can change shape and size.

Lesson 5

How are solids, liquids, and gases different?

- Solids, liquids, and gases are different from each other.
- Shape or size are ways solids, liquids, and gases can be different.

Cross-Curricular Links

English–Language Arts

Building Vocabulary

Look again at pages 4 and 5. Find the pictures for the words **property** and **solid.**

Describe some properties of a solid you see in the pictures.

Mathematics

Comparing Objects

Compare your science book with a different book.

Which book is longer?

Which book feels like it weighs more when you pick it up?

Visual and Performing Arts

Describing Art

Draw and color a picture of different kinds of fruit on a plate.

Tell about the lines, colors, and shapes you use to make the picture.

Challenge!

English–Language Arts

Describing Things

You know solids, liquids, and gases have different properties.

Write a story that describes a solid, a liquid, and a gas.

Chapter 1 Review/Test

Vocabulary

Which picture goes with each word?

1. solid (page 12)

2. liquid (page 16)

3. gas (page 18)

Think About It

4. How are solids different from liquids? (page 20)

5. How are liquids different from gases? (page 20)

6. Writing in Science Write a complete sentence. Tell the name of a liquid. (page 16)

7. Process Skills **Observe** the cover of your book. Describe one of its properties.
(pages 9,10)

8. **Use Context Clues** Which toy weighs more? (pages 14,15)

The toy that weighs more goes down.

California Standards Practice

Write the letter of the correct answer.

9. Look at the picture. Which is not a property of a beach ball?

A big

B round

C square

D smooth

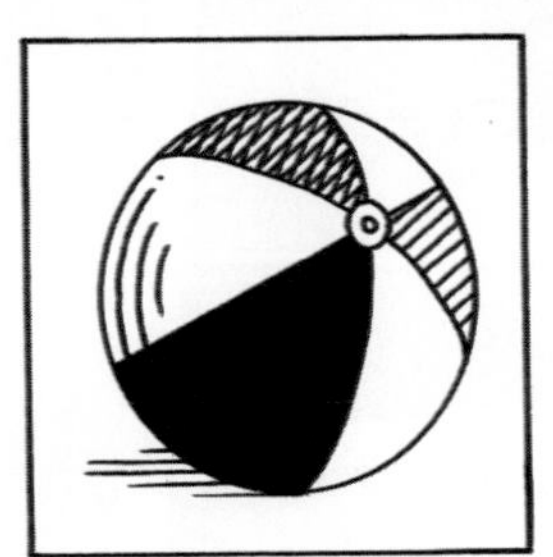

10. Which is a gas?

A blocks

B air

C water

D bricks

Weight on the Moon

Read Together

Look up in the sky at night.
You can see the Moon.
Astronauts from NASA
have walked on the Moon.

Things weigh more on
Earth than on the Moon.

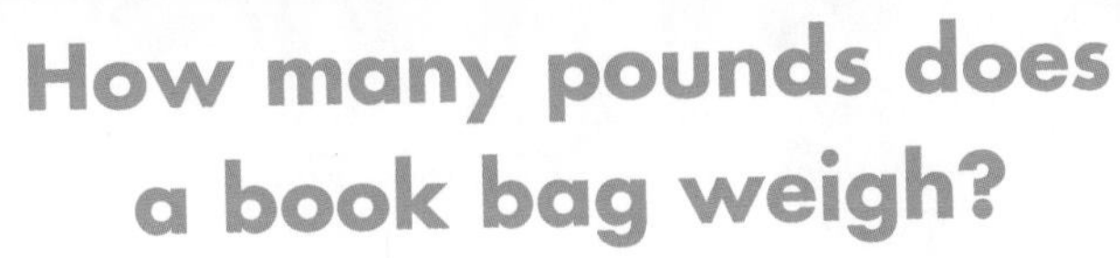

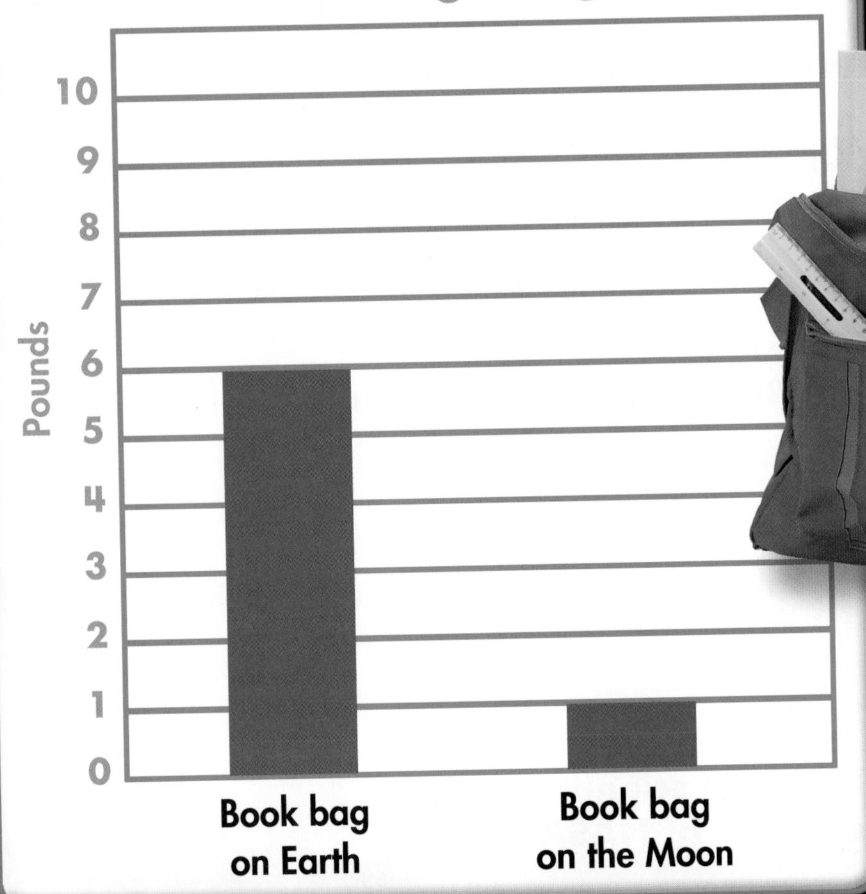

Lab zone Take-Home Activity

Draw a picture of yourself on the Moon. Show your picture to your family. Tell them why you would weigh less on the Moon.

Material Scientist

Read Together

Material scientists study the properties of different kinds of material. Some material scientists work at NASA.

Material scientists work to make things that can hold material that is very hot. Material scientists at NASA also work to make things that will not break in space.

Narrotham Bansal is a material scientist. He works at NASA.

Which can hold a spoon when it is wet? Try a tissue, a paper towel, and a piece of cloth. Tell your family what you learn.

- How can things change?
- What properties of things can change?
- What changes when things are mixed?
- How can cooling and heating change things?
- What things cannot change back?

Chapter 2

Changing Solids, Liquids, and Gases

Focus on the BIG Idea

How can things be changed?

DIGITAL g

Chapter 2
Vocabulary
melt page 40
dissolve page 45
freeze page 46
evaporate page 48
evaporate
freeze

Lab zone

Directed Inquiry

Explore How can mixing change things?

Materials

safety goggles

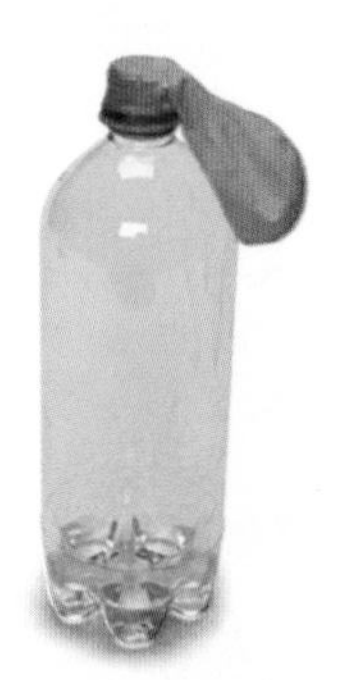

mixing bottle

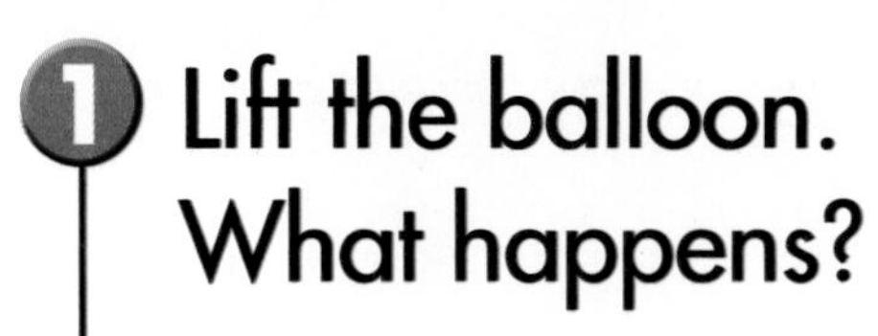

What to Do

1. Lift the balloon. What happens?
2. Draw or write what you **observe.**

Process Skills

You can **communicate** by drawing or writing what you **observe.**

Explain Your Results

Communicate Tell what you did first, next, and last. What changed?

How to Read Science

Reading Skills

Put Things in Order

To put things in order means to tell what happens first, next, and last.

Science Activity

Sand and Water

First, pour sand into a cup of water. Next, mix the sand and water together. Last, observe what happens.

Apply It!

Communicate Put in order the things to do in this science activity.

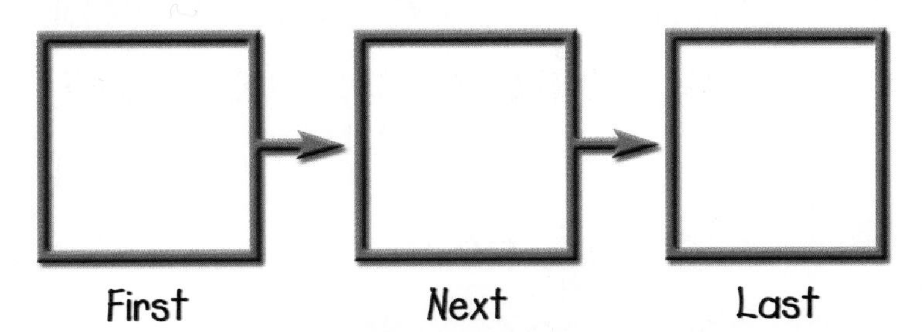

You Are There

The Crayon

Sung to the tune of "Camptown Races"
Lyrics by Gerri Brioso & Richard Freitas/The Dovetail Group, Inc.

Take solid wax and heat it up.
Heat it! Heat it!
It melts into a liquid wax
That's used to make a crayon.

Lesson 1

How can things change?

Things can change.
Some things change when they are mixed.
Some things change when they are heated or cooled.

Mixing liquid wax with red powder makes red wax.

Making Crayons

Wax is used to make crayons.
First, solid wax is heated.
Heating makes the wax change.
Heating makes the solid wax melt.
Melt means to change a solid
into a liquid.

Next, color is mixed
with the melted wax.
The wax changes to
a different color.

Plop!

Warm colored wax is poured into a mold.

Last, the colored wax is cooled. Cooling changes the melted wax back into a solid.

Wax is heated, mixed, and cooled to make crayons. Look at all the red crayons.

✓ Lesson Review

1. What happens when a solid melts?
2. TARGET SKILL **Put Things in Order** Tell how wax is changed to make crayons. Use the words first, next, and last.

Lesson 2

What properties of things can change?

Color, shape, and size are properties.
Look what happens when blue and yellow paints are mixed.
They change to a different color.

Look how the candle changes!
Wax melts when the candle is heated.
The candle gets smaller and smaller.

The candle changes size when it is heated. It changes shape too.

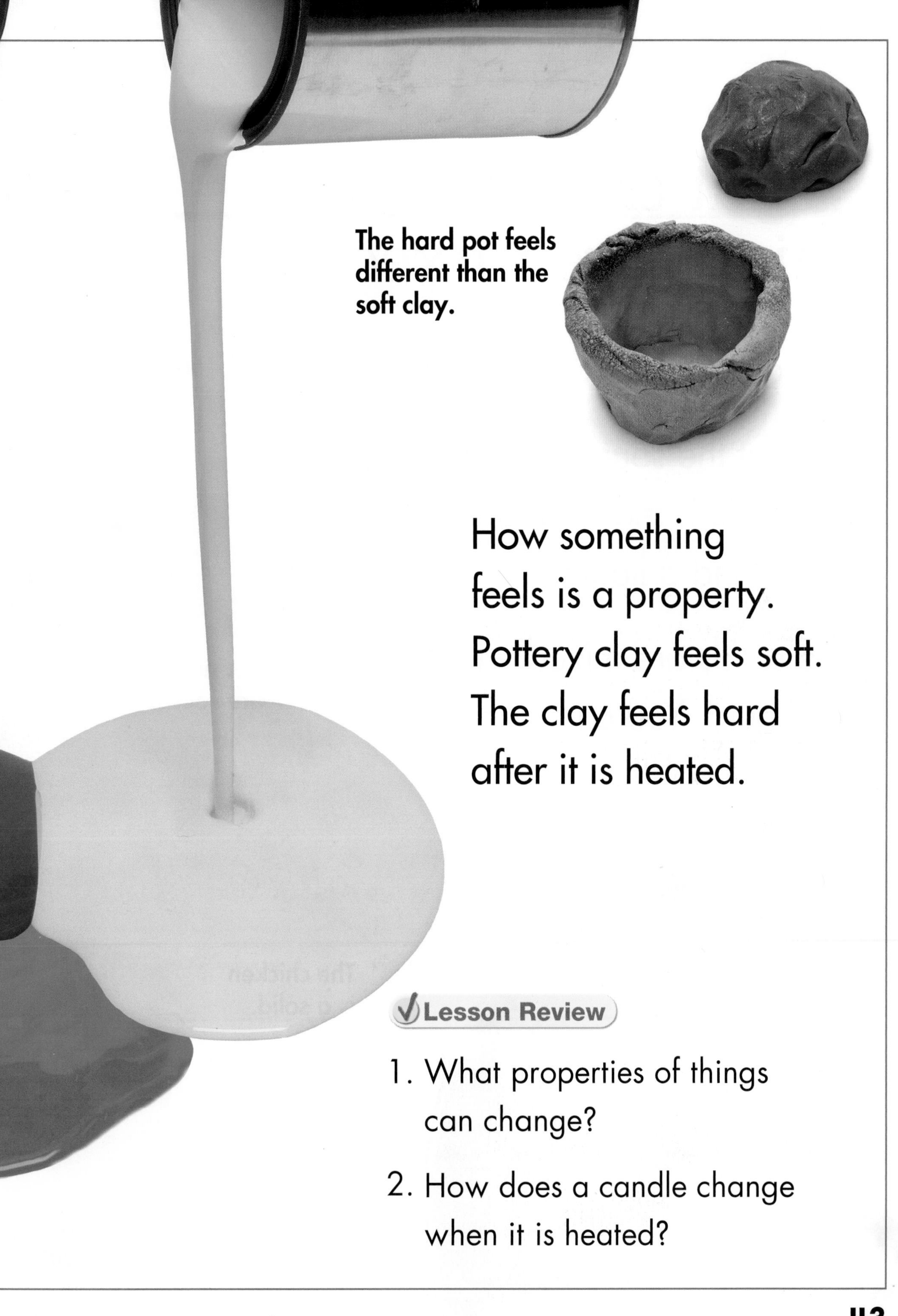

The hard pot feels different than the soft clay.

How something feels is a property. Pottery clay feels soft. The clay feels hard after it is heated.

Lesson Review

1. What properties of things can change?
2. How does a candle change when it is heated?

Lesson 3

What changes when things are mixed?

You can mix solids and liquids.

The carrots are solids.

Look at the picture. The soup is made of different solids and a liquid.

The noodles are solids.

The solids are mixed with the liquid. You can take the solids out of the liquid.

The chicken is a solid.

The broth is a liquid.

Ick!
The water now tastes salty.

Salt is a solid.
Some solids dissolve in liquids.
Dissolve means to spread throughout a liquid.
Salt dissolves when it is mixed with water.

Lesson Review

1. What happens to salt when it is mixed with water?
2. **Writing in Science** Write a complete sentence. What kinds of things are mixed to make the soup?

DIGITAL NSTA SciLinks keyword: dissolve code: gr1p45

Lesson 4

How can cooling and heating change things?

Water is a liquid.
Water can freeze when it gets very cold.
Freeze means to change from a liquid to a solid.

Frozen water is called ice.
Ice is a solid.
Ice feels cold and hard.

Brrrr!

Pour water in a tray. Freeze it to make ice.

Ice melts when it is heated.
The ice changes to water.

This water can freeze again.
It can change back to ice.

1. ✓Checkpoint How does water change when it freezes?
2. How can ice change into a liquid?

Changing Water into a Gas

Look! Everything is wet. What will happen to the water?

Water evaporates when it is heated. **Evaporate** means to change from a liquid to a gas.

Water goes into the air when it evaporates.

Heat from sunlight causes water to evaporate.

Salt dissolves in water.
The water evaporates into the air.
The salt is still there.

Mix salt with water.

Salt dissolves to make salt water.

Water evaporates. Look at the salt.

Lesson Review

1. What happens when water is heated?

2. **Put Things in Order** Look at the pictures. What happens when salt mixes with water? Use the words first, next, and last.

Lesson 5

What things can not change back?

Some things cannot change back when they are heated.

Look at the egg.
The egg cooks when it is heated.
The cooked egg cannot change back to the way it was.

Crack!
An egg changes when it is heated.

Pop!

Popcorn changes when it is heated. The popcorn cannot change back to the way it was.

✓ Lesson Review

1. What are two things that cannot change back when they are heated?
2. **Writing in Science** Write a complete sentence. Tell how an egg changes when it is heated.

Math in Science

Make a Bar Graph

Look at the objects on the page. Count how many objects are solids. Count how many objects are filled with liquid. Count how many objects are filled with gas.

Making a bar graph can help you compare what you observe. Color one box for each kind of object you see.

Number of Objects

Solid					
Liquid					
Gas					
	0	1	2	3	4 5

Use the graph to answer each question.

1. Which has the most objects?
2. Which has the least objects?

Lab zone **Take-Home Activity**

Make a bar graph. Count how many different solids, liquids, and gases you can find in a room at home.

Lab zone

Guided Inquiry

Investigate How can ice change when it melts?

Materials

cup with water

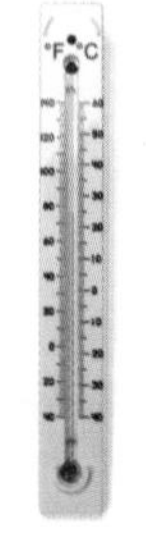
thermometer

ice cubes

clock with a second hand

What to Do

1 Observe.
Record the temperature.

A thermometer helps you see how the temperature changes.

2 Add ice. Wait 2 minutes.
Record the temperature.

The water gets cooler when you add ice.
The ice begins to melt.

Process Skills

Drawing pictures of what you **observe** can help you **communicate.**

DIGITAL Lab zone

3 Wait 1 hour. Record the temperature.

Before Ice	After Ice	
	After 2 minutes	After 1 hour
°F °C °F: 140, 120, 100, 80, 60, 40, 20, 0, 20, 40 °C: 60, 50, 40, 30, 20, 10, 0, 10, 20, 30, 40	°F °C °F: 140, 120, 100, 80, 60, 40, 20, 0, 20, 40 °C: 60, 50, 40, 30, 20, 10, 0, 10, 20, 30, 40	°F °C °F: 140, 120, 100, 80, 60, 40, 20, 0, 20, 40 °C: 60, 50, 40, 30, 20, 10, 0, 10, 20, 30, 40

Explain Your Results

1. **Communicate** How did the ice cubes change?
2. How did the temperature of the water change?

Go Further

What might happen if you started with ice water? Make a plan to find out.

Chapter 2 Reviewing Key Concepts

Focus on the BIG Idea

The properties of things can change when they are mixed, cooled, or heated.

Lesson 1

How can things change?

- Things can change when they are mixed, cooled, or heated.

Lesson 2

What properties of things can change?

- Color, size, shape, and how something feels are properties that can change.

Lesson 3

What changes when things are mixed?

- Solids can be mixed with liquids.
- Some solids dissolve when they are mixed with liquids.

Lesson 4

How can cooling and heating change things?

- Cooling can freeze water into solid ice.
- Heating can change ice back into water.
- Heating can cause water to evaporate.

Lesson 5

What things cannot change back?

- A cooked egg cannot change back to the way it was.

Cross-Curricular Links

English–Language Arts

Building Vocabulary

Look again at pages 34 and 35. Find the picture for the word **evaporate.**

Describe what happens when the water puddle evaporates.

Mathematics

Position of Objects

Look again at the pictures on page 44.

What is on the plate above and next to the cup of broth?

Visual and Performing Arts

Mixing Colors

Use markers or colored pencils to mix colors on a piece of paper. Mix red and blue. Then mix blue and yellow.

Tell a partner how the colors change.

Challenge!

English–Language Arts

Water and Sunshine

Place a small glass of water next to a window so that the Sun is shining on it. Write about what happens to the amount of water after a day. Tell what you think happens.

Chapter 2 Review/Test

Vocabulary

Which picture goes with each word?

1. melt (page 40)
2. dissolve (page 45)
3. freeze (page 46)
4. evaporate (page 48)

A

B

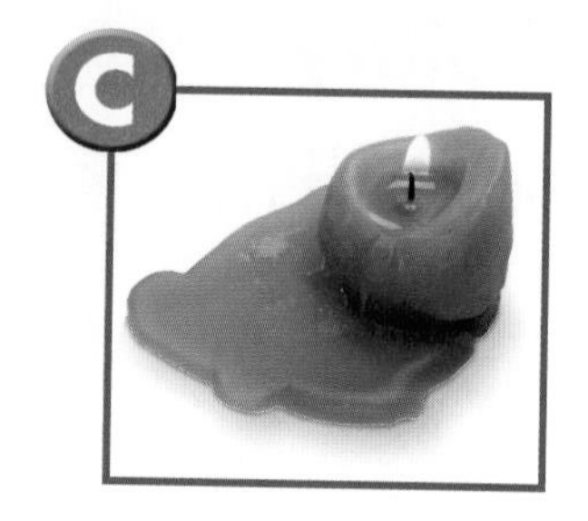

C

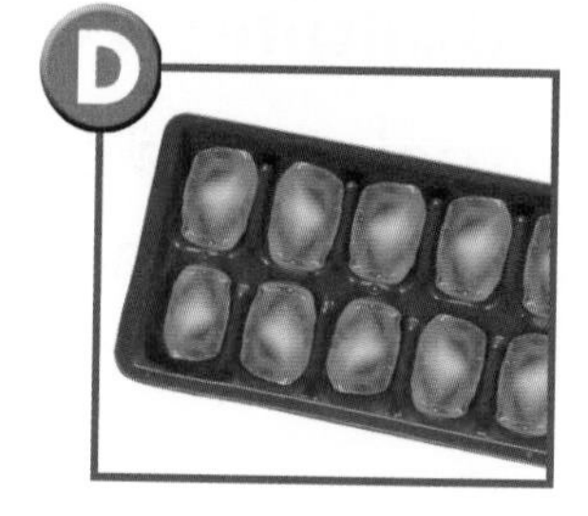

D

Think About It

5. How can things change? (page 39)
6. What properties change when a candle is heated? (page 42)

7. Writing in Science Write a sentence about how water can change. (pages 46–49)

8. Process Skills **Predict** What would happen if you left a glass of ice cubes on a table? (page 47)

9. **Put Things In Order** Tell what happens first, next, and last. (pages 48–49)

The water evaporates.
A puddle forms.
It rains.

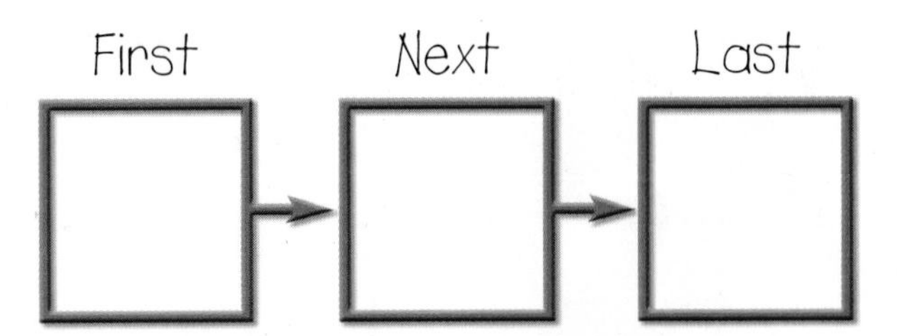

California Standards Practice

Write the letter of the correct answer.

10. What happens to water when it evaporates?

A It changes into a solid.

B It changes into a gas.

C It changes into a liquid.

D It dissolves.

11. Look at the picture. What happens when you mix salt and water?

A The salt dissolves in the water.

B The water is heated.

C The salt evaporates.

D The water and salt disappear.

Biography

Annette Baron

Read Together

Annette Baron loved art when she was young. She loved glass art the most and wondered how it was made.

When she was older she built her own glass shop. Now she teaches people how to turn hot, melted glass into beautiful art.

Annette Baron blows into the tube. The ball of glass is hot and soft.

Now the glass art is done. The glass is cool and hard.

Lab zone Take-Home Activity

Place a balloon on one end of a straw. Hold it in place using your fingers. Blow into the other end of the tube. What happens to your balloon?

Unit A Summary

Chapter 1

How can things be described?

- Solids, liquids, and gases have different properties.
- A property is something you can observe with your senses.
- Color, shape, size, weight, and how something feels are properties that can describe an object.

Chapter 2

How can things be changed?

- Solids, liquids, and gases can change when they are mixed, cooled, or heated.
- Some things that change can be changed back to the way they were.
- Some things that change cannot be changed back to the way they were.

Show What You Know

Write and Sing a Song

- Make up a song about ice changing to water and water changing back to ice.
- Sing your song to the class.

Make a Card Game

- Draw pictures on cards.
- Make 2 cards that show a solid, 2 cards that show a liquid, and 2 cards that show a gas.
- Mix the cards. Then have a partner match the cards that show the same kinds of things.

Write a Poem

Write a poem about a solid, liquid, or gas. Tell about its color, shape, size, and weight. Tell how it feels.

Read More About Physical Sciences

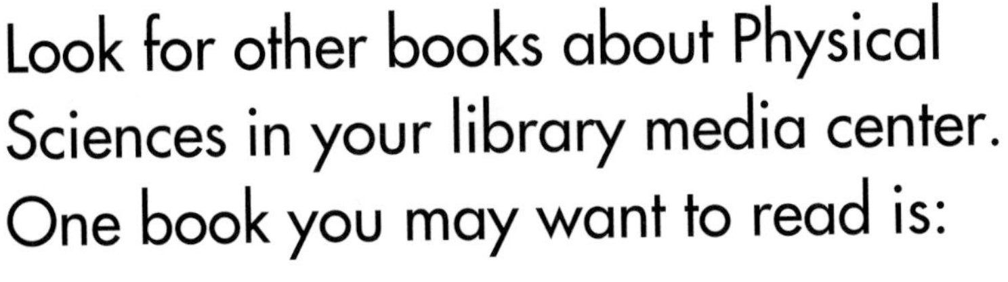

Look for other books about Physical Sciences in your library media center. One book you may want to read is:

Splish Splash
by Joan Bransfield Graham

This book has poems and pictures about different forms of water, from ice cubes to the ocean.

Discovery Channel School

Science Fair Projects

Full Inquiry

Using Scientific Methods

1. Ask a question.
2. Make a hypothesis.
3. Plan a fair test.
4. Do your test.
5. Record what happens.
6. Tell your conclusions.
7. Go further.

Idea 1

How Water Evaporates

Plan a project.
Find out if water evaporates faster in the sunlight or in the shade.

Idea 2

Cooling a Balloon

Plan a project.
Find out if the size of a balloon changes when it is put in cold water.

Unit A California Standards Practice

Write the letter of the correct answer.

1. What is a property?

A a liquid
B a solid
C an object
D something about an object that you can observe

2. Which tells about a gas?

A A gas has its own shape.
B A gas does not change size.
C A gas can change size and shape.
D You can see most gases.

3. Look at the picture. The vase is filled with liquid. Which answer tells about a liquid?

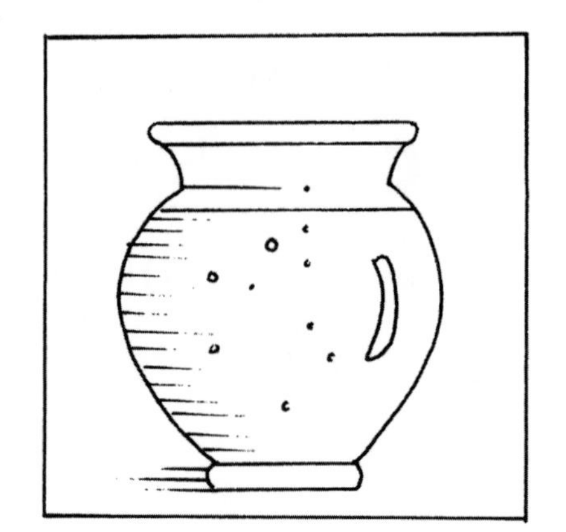

A It takes the shape of its container.

B It can change its size.

C It cannot change its shape.

D It cannot be seen.

4. Which answer tells about a solid?

A It takes the shape of its container.

B It has its own shape and size.

C It takes the size of its container.

D It is always blue.

Unit A California Standards Practice

5. What happens when water freezes?

A It changes into a gas.
B It changes into a solid.
C It changes into a liquid.
D It is called hot water.

6. What happens to an egg when it is heated?

A It changes to a liquid and can change back.
B It changes to a gas and can change back.
C It changes to a solid and can change back.
D It changes to a solid and cannot change back.

Unit A California Standards Practice

7. What does evaporate mean?

A to change from a solid to a liquid
B to change from a gas to a solid
C to change from a liquid to a gas
D to change from a gas to a liquid

8. What happens when salt dissolves?

A It spreads throughout a liquid.
B It becomes part of a solid.
C It becomes part of a gas.
D It sinks to the bottom of a liquid.

CALIFORNIA Unit B

Life Sciences

California Field Trip

Malibu Creek State Park

Los Angeles, California

Malibu Creek State Park is only 25 miles from Los Angeles. It is in the middle of the Santa Monica Mountains. Many birds, insects, and other animals find food and shelter in the park.

Find Out More

Research to find out more about Malibu Creek State Park.

- Make a list of some plants and animals you can see at the park.

Los Angeles

- What do plants need?
- How do plants get what they need?
- What do animals need?

Chapter 3

Needs of Plants and Animals

What do plants and animals need?

Chapter 3
Vocabulary
living page 79
roots page 83
nutrients page 83
leaves page 84
living
leaves

Lab zone

Directed Inquiry

Explore Do plants need water?

Materials

bowl with gravel

bowl with gravel and water

bean seeds

magnifier

What to Do

1. Put 4 bean seeds on the gravel in each bowl.

no water

water

What do seeds grow to be?

2. **Observe** for 4 days.

Explain Your Results

1. Draw what happens.
2. **Infer** Can a plant grow without water?

Process Skills

You can use what you **observe** to **infer.**

How to Read Science

Reading Skills

Relate Prior Knowledge

Relate prior knowledge means to use what you know already about a topic.

Science Story

Grassland

These animals live in a grassland. Animals need food and water to live. They need food and water to grow and change.

Apply It!

Infer Look at the picture. Why do you think the animals have come to the water hole?

Tell what I know.

You Are There

Living Things

Sung to the tune of "Found a Peanut"
Lyrics by Gerri Brioso & Richard Freitas/The Dovetail Group, Inc.

Plants are living things. So are animals.
So are people, yes we know.
Living things need food and water.
Living things all change and grow.

Lesson 1

What do plants need?

Living things are alive.
Plants are living things.
Plants can grow and change.
Living things have needs.

This deer is a living thing too.

What Plants Need

A need is something a living thing must have to live. Plants need air to live. Plants need water.

Plants need light too. Plants get light from the Sun. Plants need light to grow and change.

Rain can give plants the water they need.

The Sun gives these plants the light they need to grow.

Lesson Review

1. What do plants need to live?
2. **Relate Prior Knowledge** Tell what might happen if a plant does not get light.

TARGET SKILL

Lesson 2

How do plants get what they need?

Many plants have the same parts.
These parts help a plant get what it needs.
These parts help a plant live and grow.

These plants have parts.

Most plants have roots.
Roots hold a plant
in the ground.
Roots take in water
from the soil.
Roots take in nutrients
from the soil.

Nutrients are materials
that living things need.

1. **Checkpoint** What are nutrients?
2. **Relate Prior Knowledge** Tell how the roots help a plant get what it needs to live.

TARGET SKILL

DIGITAL NSTA SciLinks keyword: roots code: gr1p83

Lesson 3

What do animals need?

You learned that living things are alive.
Animals are living things.
Animals can grow and change.
Animals have needs too.

Munch!

Bears need food to live.

Animals need air to live.
Animals need water to live.
Animals need food too.
Animals get energy from food.

Lesson Review

1. What do animals need to live?
2. Tell why a bear is a living thing.

Slurp!

Bears need water to live.

Math in Science

TALLYING

You can use tally marks to record information.

| This is a tally mark.

𝍸 These are 5 tally marks.

Plant	Tally	Total
Tree	𝍸 |	6
Flower		

This chart shows how many trees are in the circle.

Make tally marks to record how many flowers are in the circle. Then write the total.

Make tally marks to record how many birds, lizards and insects there are in the picture. Then write the totals.

Animals	Tally	Total
Bird		
Lizard		
Insect		

1. Which animal has the greatest number?
2. Which animal has the smallest number?

Lab zone **Take-Home Activity**

Make a tally chart. Record the number of plants and animals you can find around home.

Chapter 3 Reviewing Key Concepts

Focus on the BIG Idea

Both plants and animals need water and air. Animals need food. Plants need light to make food.

Lesson 1

What do plants need?

- Plants need air, water, and light to live.
- Plants get light from the Sun.

Lesson 2

How do plants get what they need?

- Roots take in water and nutrients from the soil.
- Green leaves take in energy from sunlight and make food for the plant.

Lesson 3

What do animals need?

- Animals need water and air to live.
- Animals need food too.

Cross-Curricular Links

English–Language Arts

Building Vocabulary

Look again at pages 74 and 75. Find the picture for the word **leaves.**

Write about the color of these leaves. Tell what leaves do for the plant.

Mathematics

Planning a Garden

Suppose you have 8 plants to make a garden.

Make a picture to show how you can put all the plants in 2 rows. Each row should have the same number of plants.

Visual and Performing Arts

Drawing a Leaf

Look at a leaf. Draw and color a picture of the leaf.

Make your picture the same size, shape, and color as the leaf.

Challenge!

Health

Eating Vegetables

You need good food to stay healthy. Vegetables help you get the vitamins you need.

Research and make a list of vegetables to eat.

Chapter 1 Review/Test

Vocabulary

Which picture goes with each word?

1. roots (page 83)

2. leaves (page 84)

Think About It

3. What are two kinds of living things? (pages 79, 86)

4. What part of the plant takes in water and nutrients from the soil? (page 83)

5. Why do animals need to eat? (page 87)

6. Writing in Science Name three things animals need to live. (page 87)

7. Process Skills **Infer** What might happen if a plant does not get the light and water it needs? (page 80)

8. **Relate Prior Knowledge** What part of the plant takes in sunlight? (page 85)

Plants have parts that help them live and grow.

Tell what I know.

California Standards Practice

Write the letter of the correct answer.

9. What part of the plant makes food?

A flowers

B leaves

C stems

D roots

10. What are nutrients?

A parts of a plant that take in water

B materials that living things need

C living things

D light from the Sun

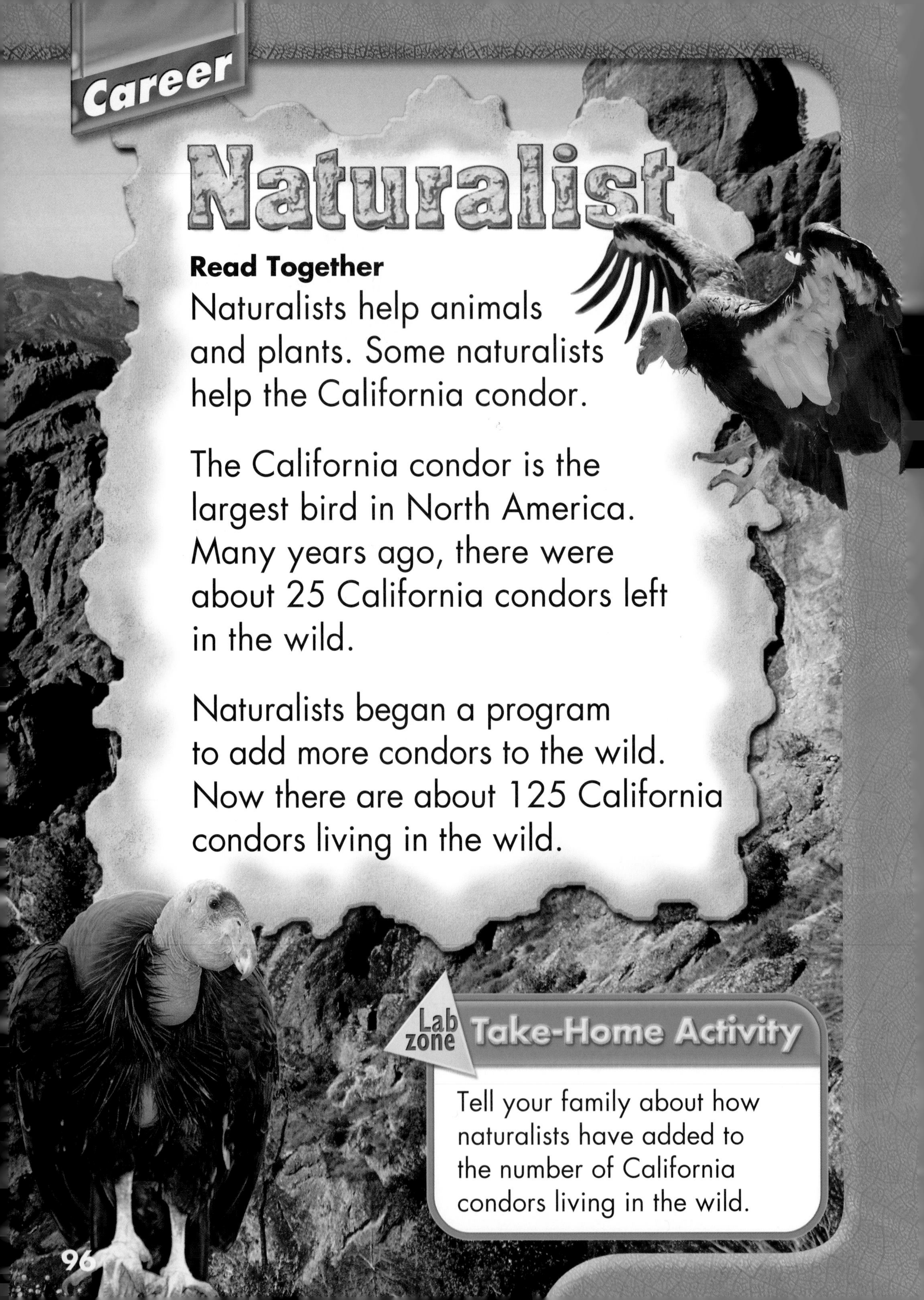

Career

Naturalist

Read Together

Naturalists help animals and plants. Some naturalists help the California condor.

The California condor is the largest bird in North America. Many years ago, there were about 25 California condors left in the wild.

Naturalists began a program to add more condors to the wild. Now there are about 125 California condors living in the wild.

Lab zone Take-Home Activity

Tell your family about how naturalists have added to the number of California condors living in the wild.

- What is an environment?
- What lives in a forest?
- What lives in an ocean?
- What lives in a desert?

Chapter 4
Environments

Focus on the BIG Idea
Where do plants and animals live?
environment
ocean
forest
DIGITAL
g

Chapter 4 Vocabulary

Lab zone

Directed Inquiry

Explore Where do animals live?

Materials

yarn

picture cards

land

word cards

What to Do

1. Make 2 yarn circles.

2. Sort the picture cards.
   Which animals live on land?
   Which animals live in water?

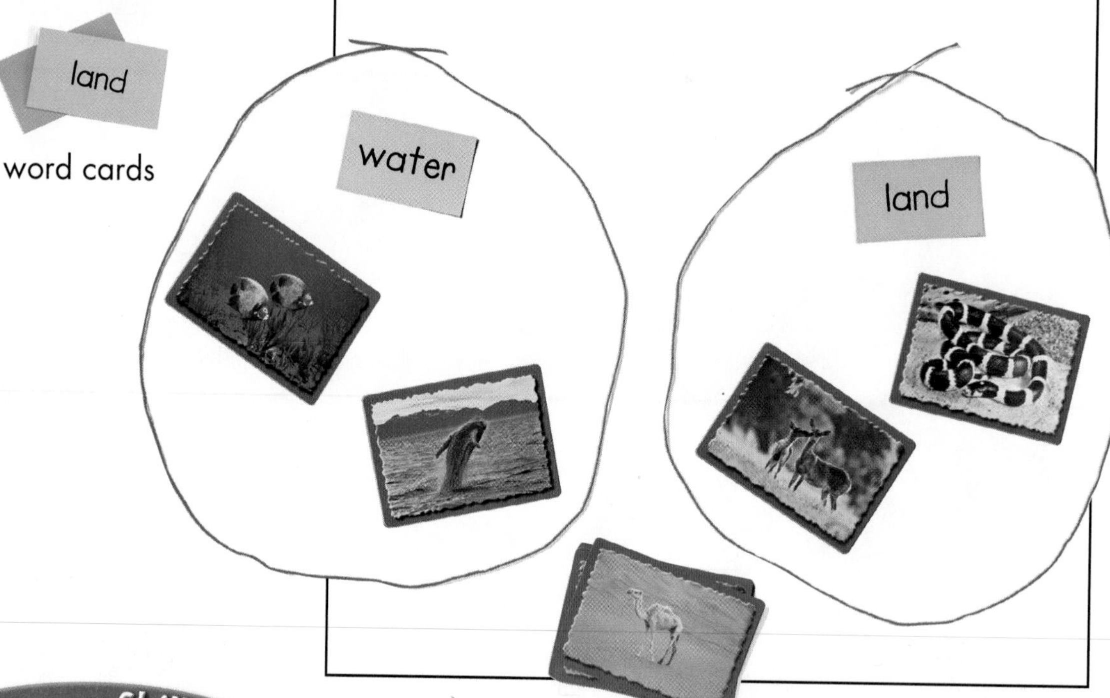

Explain Your Results

Classify two more animals.
Draw them.

Process Skills

Classify means to sort things that are alike and different.

DIGITAL Lab zone

How to Read Science

Reading Skills

Use Context Clues

Pictures can give you clues about what you read.

Science Story

Different animals live in different places. The sea otter has thick fur that keeps it warm in water. The black bear has thick fur that keeps it warm on land.

Apply It!

Classify Where can different animals with fur live?

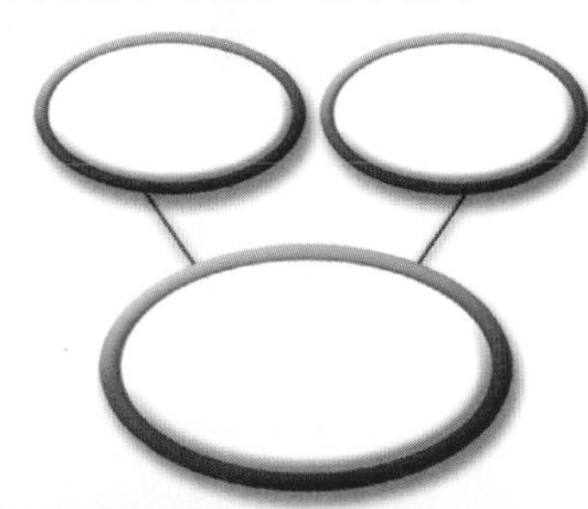

You Are There

DIGITAL

Environments

Sung to the tune of "Mary Had A Little Lamb"
Lyrics by Gerri Brioso & Richard Freitas/The Dovetail Group, Inc.

A forest is an environment
With big tall trees
And lots of plants.
A forest is an environment
For different animals.

DIGITAL

Lesson 1

What is an environment?

An **environment** is a place where plants and animals live.

An environment has food and water.
An environment has air.

An environment gives plants and animals what they need to live.

This raccoon finds food and water where it lives.

Living in an Environment

Plants and animals have parts you can see. The parts help plants and animals to live in their environment.

Clip Clop! This sheep lives where it is rocky. The sheep has hooves to climb on rocks.

This plant does not get much sunlight. It has big leaves that take in more of the sunlight it gets.

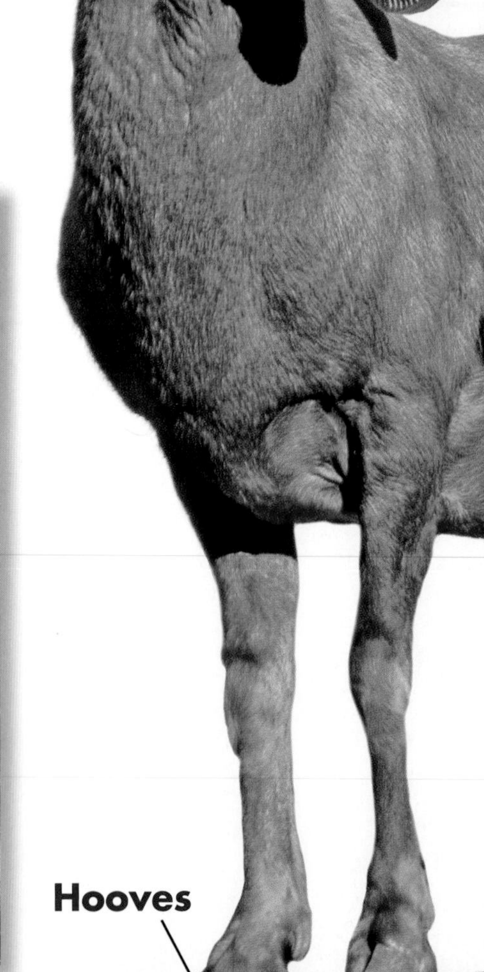

Giraffes have long necks. Giraffes can reach the leaves high in a tree.

Long necks help giraffes see animals that may hurt them too.

See the giraffe eat leaves.

1. What is an environment?

2. **Use Context Clues** What body part helps a giraffe reach leaves in trees? Look for clues in the picture.

Lesson 2

What lives in a forest?

A forest is an environment.
A **forest** has many trees and other plants.
Some forests get cold in winter.

This plant grows in a forest.

Trees have different kinds of leaves.
Some trees have flat leaves.
Some trees have leaves that
look like needles.

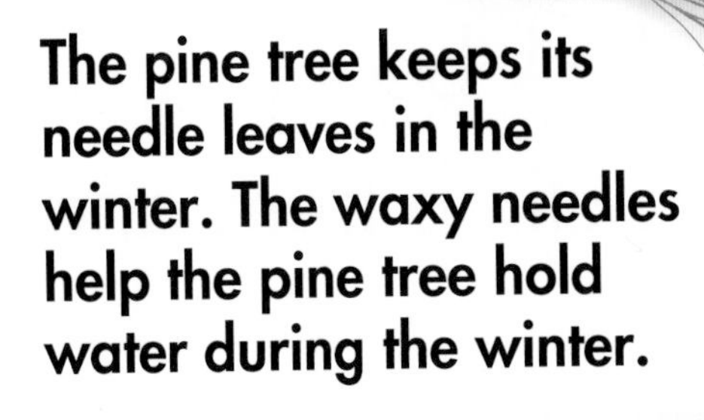

The pine tree keeps its needle leaves in the winter. The waxy needles help the pine tree hold water during the winter.

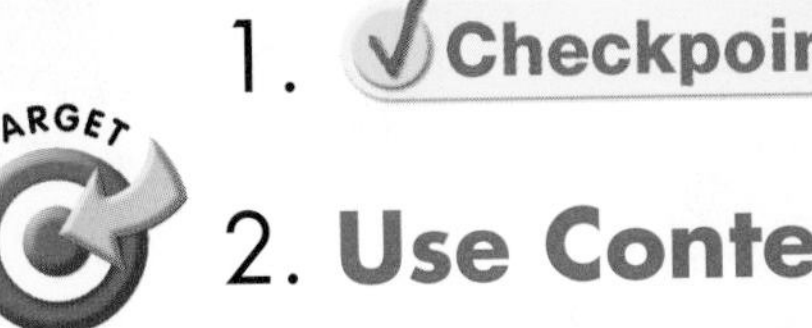

1. ✓ Checkpoint What is a forest?
2. **Use Context Clues** What property of pine tree leaves help the tree live in winter?

Animals Living in Forests

Many animals live in forests.
Black bears live in forests.
Black bears have sharp claws.
Black bears can use their claws
to climb trees and to get food.

Scratch!

This baby bear has sharp claws.

Black bears have thick fur too. The fur keeps black bears warm in the forest.

Rat-a-tat-tat!

This woodpecker uses its bill to make holes in trees. The woodpecker puts acorns in the holes to eat in winter.

Lesson Review

1. What body parts does a black bear have that help it live in a forest?

2. **Writing in Science** Describe how a woodpecker uses its bill to live in a forest.

Lesson 3

What lives in an ocean?

An ocean is an environment.
An **ocean** is a large body of salt water.
Many animals and plants live in an ocean.
Some parts of an ocean are deep.

Surfgrass is an ocean plant. Surfgrass has roots, stems, leaves, and flowers. Many animals live in surfgrass.

This sea urchin has sharp spines. The spines protect it from other animals in the ocean.

Gulp!

This fish lives in the ocean. The fish has gills to breathe in water.

1. ✓Checkpoint What is an ocean?
2. What is one kind of ocean plant?

Other Animals in an Ocean Environment

Splish splash! Look at the sea otter!
Thick fur keeps the sea otter warm.
A sea otter drinks salt water.
A sea otter finds food in the ocean too.

A sea otter can rest by floating on its back.

An albatross has very long wings. An albatross uses its wings to fly for a long time over an ocean.

A gray whale has thick fat called blubber. The blubber helps to keep it warm in an ocean.

Lesson Review

1. What body part helps an albatross live in an ocean environment?
2. Tell about the body parts that help keep sea otters and gray whales warm.

Lesson 4

What lives in a desert?

A desert is an environment.
A **desert** is very dry.
Many plants and animals live in the desert.

A desert gets lots of sunlight.
A desert gets very little rain.
Deserts may get hot during the day.

This bush has small waxy leaves. The leaves help the plant keep its water in a desert.

Ouch!

This cactus has sharp spines. The spines protect the cactus from animals that may eat it.

1. ✓ Checkpoint What is a desert?
2. What part of the cactus helps protect it from animals?

Animals in a Desert

A desert iguana has light colored skin.
Light colors stay cooler in the hot Sun.
The light skin helps the iguana keep cool.

Look at the color of this desert iguana.

Zoom!

The roadrunner has long legs. It can run very fast to catch food.

Shhh!

This rabbit has long ears that help it keep cool. It can hear other animals when they are near.

Lesson Review

1. What helps a desert iguana keep cool in the desert?
2. **Writing in Science** Tell how the roadrunner gets food in the desert.

Math in Science

Comparing Animals

Look at the pictures. Make a bar graph to show how many animals are in each picture.

	Number of Animals	
6		
5		
4		
3		
2		
1		
0	forest	desert

Lab zone Take-Home Activity

Choose an environment. Draw plants and animals that live in the environment. Make a bar graph to show how many plants and animals are in your picture.

Chapter 4 Reviewing Key Concepts

Focus on the BIG Idea Different plants and animals have different parts that help them live in different environments.

Lesson 1

What is an environment?

- An environment is a place where plants and animals live.
- Plants and animals have parts that help them live in their environment.

Lesson 2

What lives in a forest?

- A forest is an environment.
- Many different plants and animals have parts that help them to live in a forest.

Lesson 3

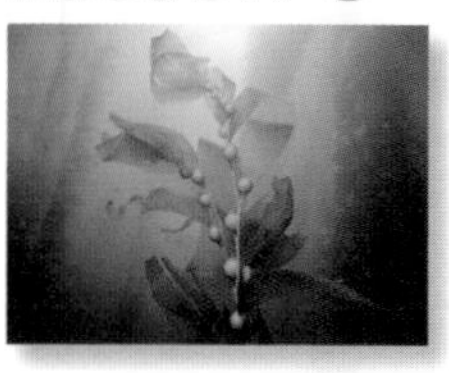

What lives in an ocean?

- An ocean is an environment.
- Many different plants and animals have parts that help them to live in an ocean.

Lesson 4

What lives in a desert?

- A desert is an environment.
- Many different plants and animals have parts that help them to live in a desert.

Cross-Curricular Links

English–Language Arts

Building Vocabulary

Look again at pages 98 and 99. Find the pictures for the words **environment** and **forest.**

Write a sentence using the two words.

Mathematics

Numbering Wolves

Look back at page 118. Find the picture of the wolves. Suppose 5 more wolves join the pack.

How many wolves would there be in all?

Health

Staying Safe in the Sun

Tian made a list of healthy things he does when he plays in the Sun. Act out one of the things Tian does. Have a partner guess what it is. Take turns.

Sunny Environment
1. Use sunscreen.
2. Wear a hat.

Challenge!

English–Language Arts

Living in a Desert

Suppose you are in a desert. Write a story about a plant and an animal.

Tell about parts you can see that help the plant and animal to live in the desert.

Chapter 4 Review/Test

Vocabulary

Which picture goes with each word?

1. forest (page 106)

2. ocean (page 110)

3. desert (page 114)

A

B

C

Think About It

4. What are the parts of a surfgrass plant? (page 110)

5. How does the skin color of the desert iguana help it to live in the desert? (page 116)

6. **Writing in Science** Tell about a body part that helps a black bear live in a forest. (page 108)

7. **Process Skills** **Classify** Which animals belong in a forest and which in an ocean? (pages 108–113)

Whale

Bear

Woodpecker

Fish

8. **Use Context Clues**

Where does the plant live?

(page 114)

Small waxy leaves help this plant keep water in a desert.

California Standards Practice

Write the letter of the correct answer.

9. Where do all plants and animals live?

A in a desert

B in an ocean

C in an environment

D in a forest

10. Look at the picture. What body part helps this sheep live in its environment?

A feathers to keep it warm

B blubber to keep it warm

C a long neck to reach leaves

D hooves to climb on rocks

Dr. Sonia Ortega

Read Together

Dr. Sonia Ortega liked to look for insects when she was young. When she grew up she wanted to learn more about other animals.

Dr. Ortega became a marine biologist. She studied how oysters live in the ocean. She wanted to learn where oysters grow the best.

Dr. Ortega knows that scientists must ask good questions and do careful studies to learn more.

Lab zone Take-Home Activity

Look for a place where plants and animals live near your home. Draw a picture of the place.

Standards Focus Questions

- How do plants and animals need one another?
- How do animals help spread seeds?
- What is a food chain?
- How do living things get food in a desert?
- How do living things get food in a marsh?
- What do animals eat?

Chapter 5

Plants and Animals Living Together

How do plants and animals live together?

Chapter 5 Vocabulary

Lab zone Directed Inquiry

Explore What do animals eat for food?

Materials

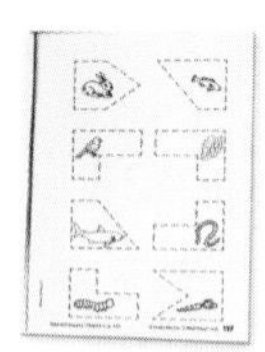

Matching Cards

scissors

crayons or markers

glue

construction paper

What to Do

1. Cut out the cards. Color the picture.
2. Match the cards.
Show what each animal eats.
3. Glue the cards onto your paper.

Process Skills

You use what you know and what you observe when you **infer.**

Explain Your Results

Infer What kinds of things do animals eat?

How to Read Science

Reading Skills

Predict

Predict means to tell what you think might happen next. Look for words that tell you what will happen.

Science Story

What Sharks Eat

Sharks eat other fish for food. Soon the shark will eat the fish.

Apply It!

Infer What do you think the shark will eat? Read the story to find out.

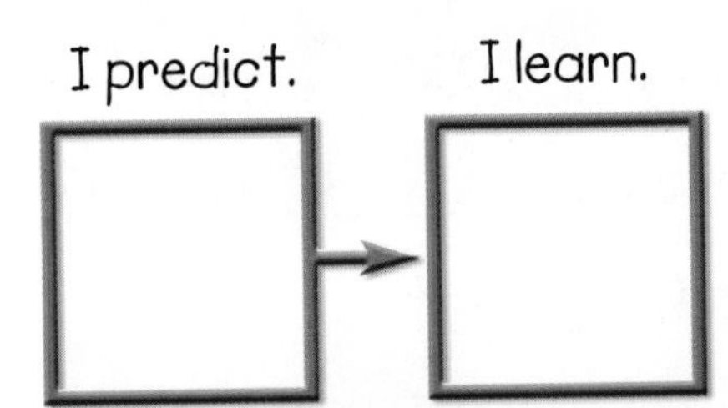

You Are There

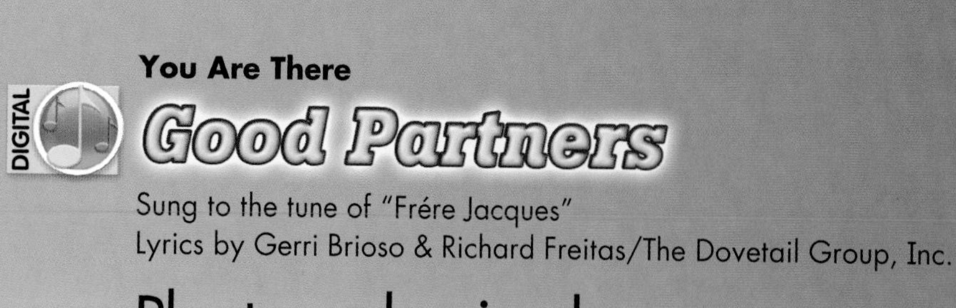

Good Partners

Sung to the tune of "Frére Jacques"
Lyrics by Gerri Brioso & Richard Freitas/The Dovetail Group, Inc.

Plants and animals,
Are good partners.
Yes, they are.
Yes, they are.
Plants can be a shelter,
For animals to live in.
That's a fact.
That's a fact.

Lesson 1

How do plants and animals need one another?

Did you know that plants and animals need each other to live? Plants grow almost everywhere in the world.

Some animals eat plants for food. Some animals eat other animals. Some animals make nests in plants. Some animals even make nests on other animals.

Some birds build nests in grasses.

Animals Need Shelter

Many animals use plants for shelter.
A **shelter** is a safe place for animals to live.
Some animals build nests for shelter.
Some animals use trees for shelter.

Some birds build nests in shrubs.

Some birds build nests in trees.

Some squirrels u trees as shelter.

Some animals use other animals for shelter.
Fleas use other animals for shelter.

Lesson Review

1. What is a shelter?
2. **Writing in Science** Write a sentence. Tell where animals might nest or find shelter.

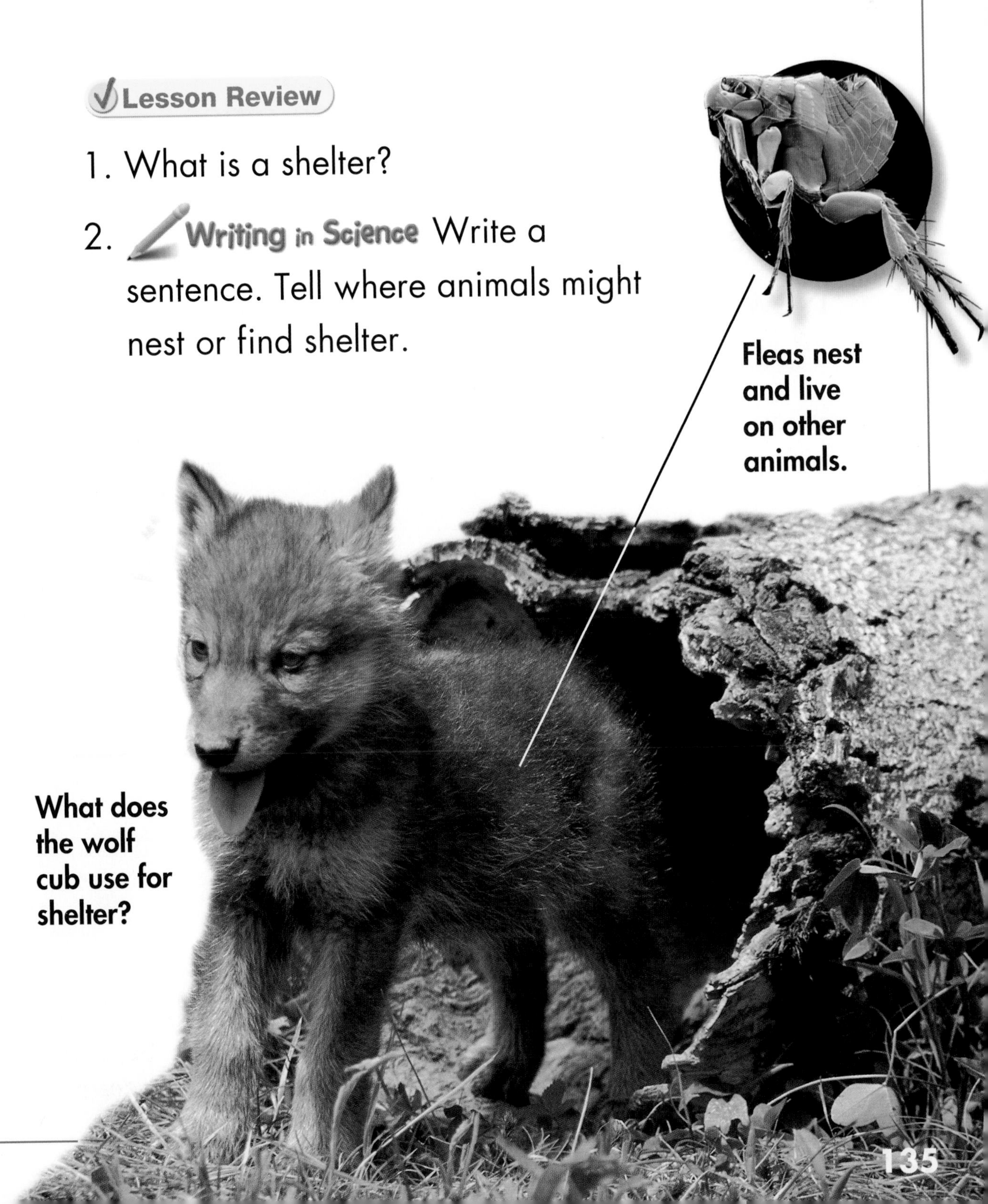

Fleas nest and live on other animals.

What does the wolf cub use for shelter?

Lesson 2

How do animals help spread seeds?

Plants and animals need each other.
Some animals spread plant seeds.
Some animals carry seeds to new places.
New plants may grow from these seeds.

Seeds might stick to the fur on the bear. The bear moves the seeds to new places.

The squirrel carries an acorn to a new place.

The acorn might grow into a new oak tree.

Squirrels bury some acorns in the ground.
Oak trees may grow from these acorns.

Birds drop and spread seeds too.

Lesson Review

1. How do some animals help plants?
2. **Writing in Science** Write two sentences to tell how animals might spread seeds.

Lesson 3

What is a food chain?

You know plants use energy from sunlight to make food.
You know some animals eat plants.
Then other animals eat those animals.
This is called a **food chain.**
Look at one kind of food chain.

This plant uses sunlight to make food. A caterpillar eats the leaf for food.

Plants and animals depend on each other through food chains.

Lesson Review

1. What do animals eat for food?
2. **Predict** What might eat the bird?

Yum!

The bird eats the caterpillar for food.

Lesson 4

How do living things get food in a desert?

You know that a desert is an environment.
There are food chains in a desert.
Desert plants use energy from sunlight to make food.
Some insects eat the plants for food.

This shrub grows in the desert.

Crunch!
The insect eats the leaves of the desert shrub.

The lizard sees the insect.
The hungry lizard eats
the insect for food.

Zap!
The lizard will catch the insect.

1. Checkpoint What does the lizard eat for food?
2. What might an animal in a desert eat?

Food for Desert Animals

The roadrunner sees the lizard.
The roadrunner eats the lizard for food.
The coyote sees the roadrunner.
The coyote eats the roadrunner for food.

Gulp!
The roadrunner will eat the lizard.

DIGITAL Look for Active Art animations at www.pearsonsuccessnet.com

Pounce!

The coyote will catch the roadrunner.

Lesson Review

1. What does the coyote eat?

2. How does a shrub get food in a desert?

coyote

roadrunner

lizard

insect

shrub takes in sunlight

Lesson 5

How do living things get food in a marsh?

There are food chains in a marsh.
A **marsh** is a wetland environment.
Tall grass grows in a marsh.
The grass uses energy from sunlight to make food.
The cricket eats the grass for food.

Snap!
The cricket bites the grass.

Ribbit!

The frog will catch and eat the cricket.

The hungry frog
eats the cricket for food.

1. ✓Checkpoint What does the cricket eat?
2. What might animals in a marsh eat?

Food for Marsh Animals

The hungry snake sees the frog.
The snake moves toward the frog.

The hungry hawk sees the snake. The hawk flies toward the snake.

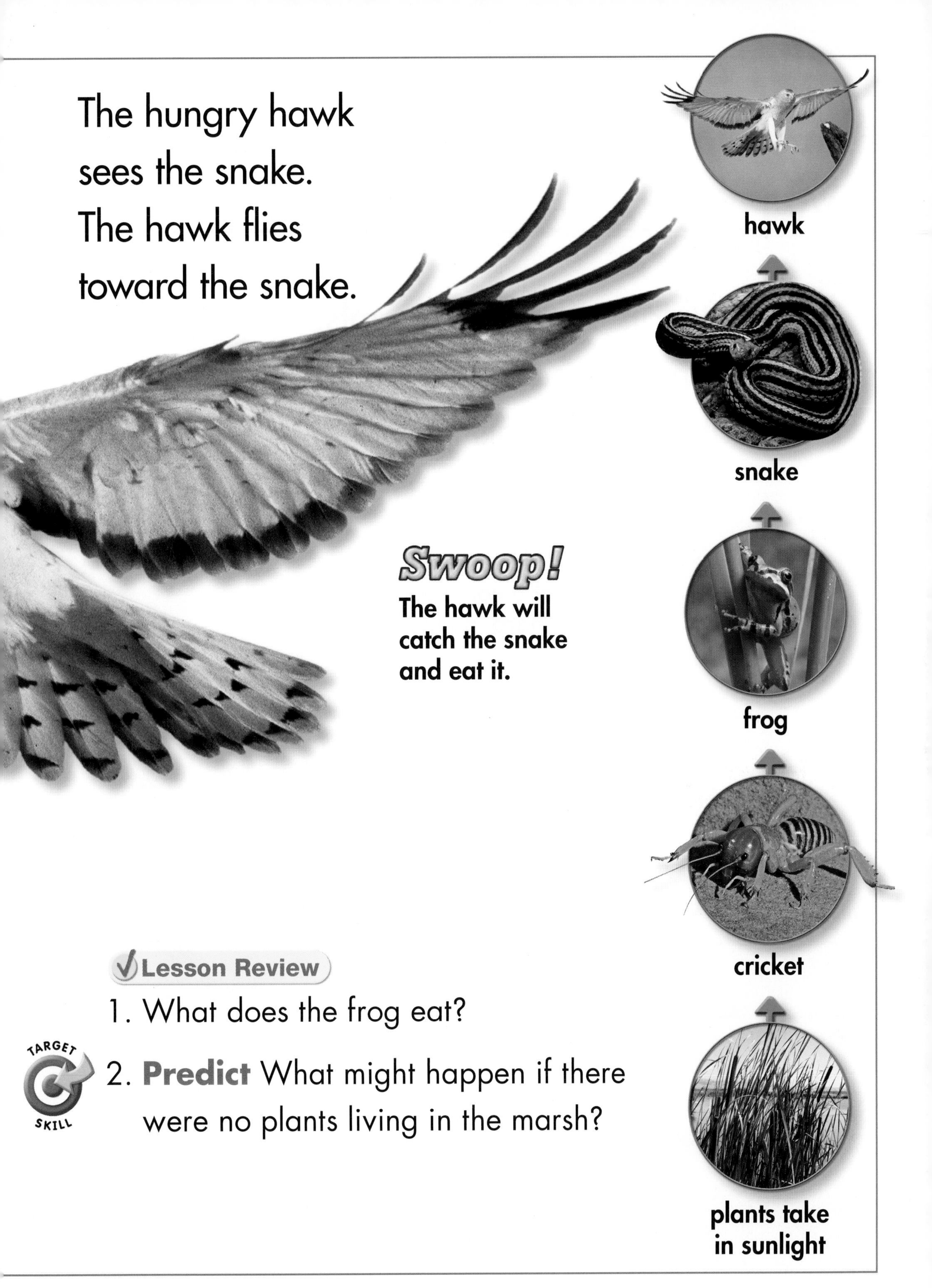

Swoop!

The hawk will catch the snake and eat it.

Lesson Review

1. What does the frog eat?
2. **Predict** What might happen if there were no plants living in the marsh?

TARGET SKILL

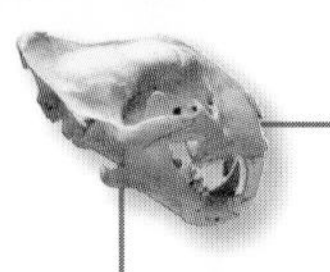

Lesson 6

What do animals eat?

Some animals eat other animals.
Wolves and crocodiles eat other animals.
Lions eat other animals too.

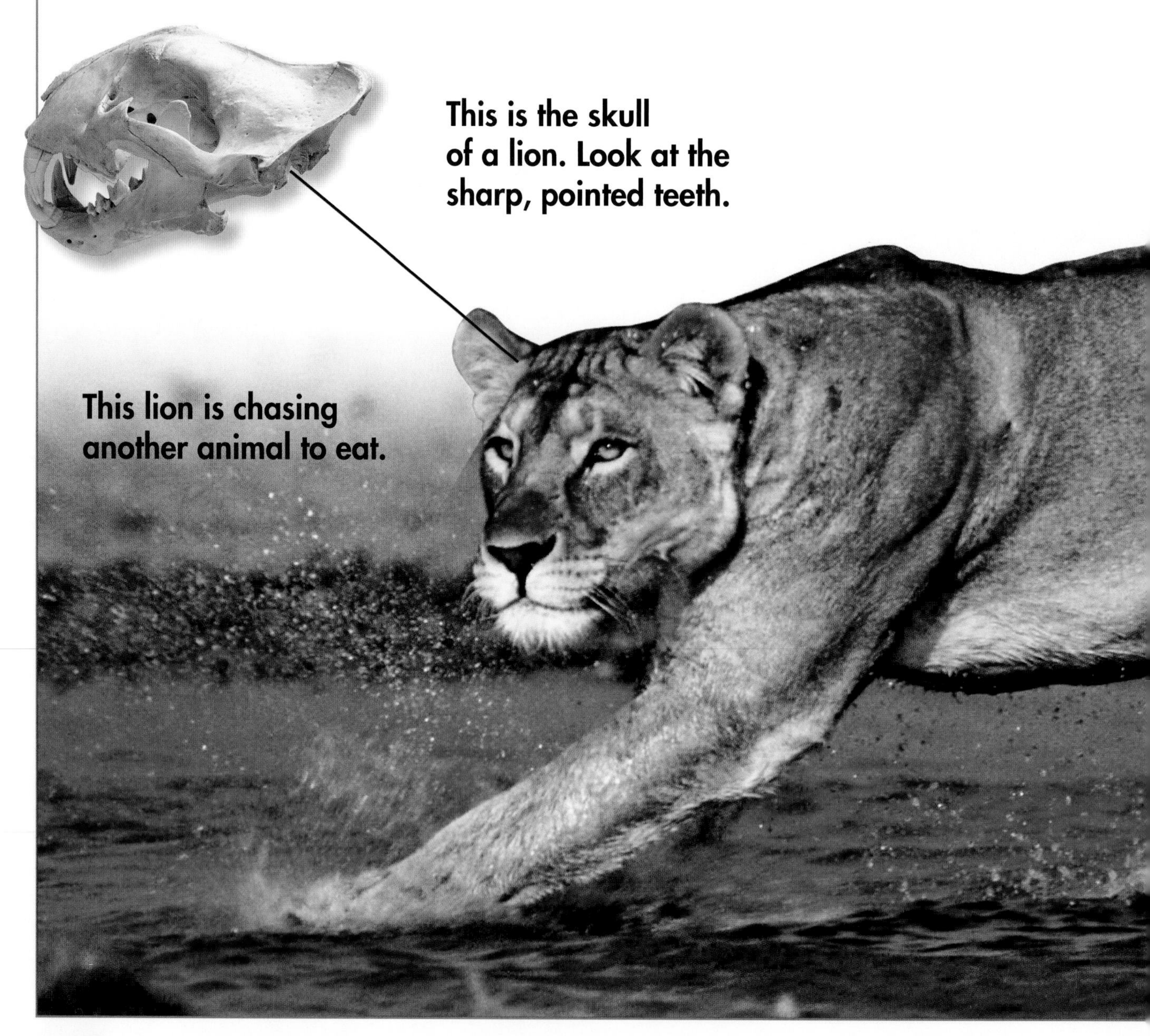

This is the skull of a lion. Look at the sharp, pointed teeth.

This lion is chasing another animal to eat.

A lion has sharp, pointed teeth. Sharp, pointed teeth can rip and tear meat.

How can you tell what animals eat?
You can look at their teeth.
Many animals that eat other animals have sharp, pointed teeth.

1. Checkpoint What do lions eat for food?
2. Writing in Science How can you tell what lions eat?

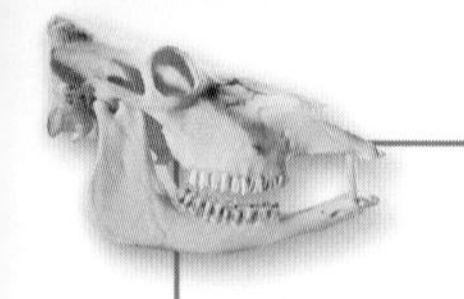

Animals that Eat Plants

Many animals eat plants for food.
Deer and squirrels eat plants.
Cows eat plants too.

Crunch!
This cow eats grass.

Many animals that eat plants have flat teeth.

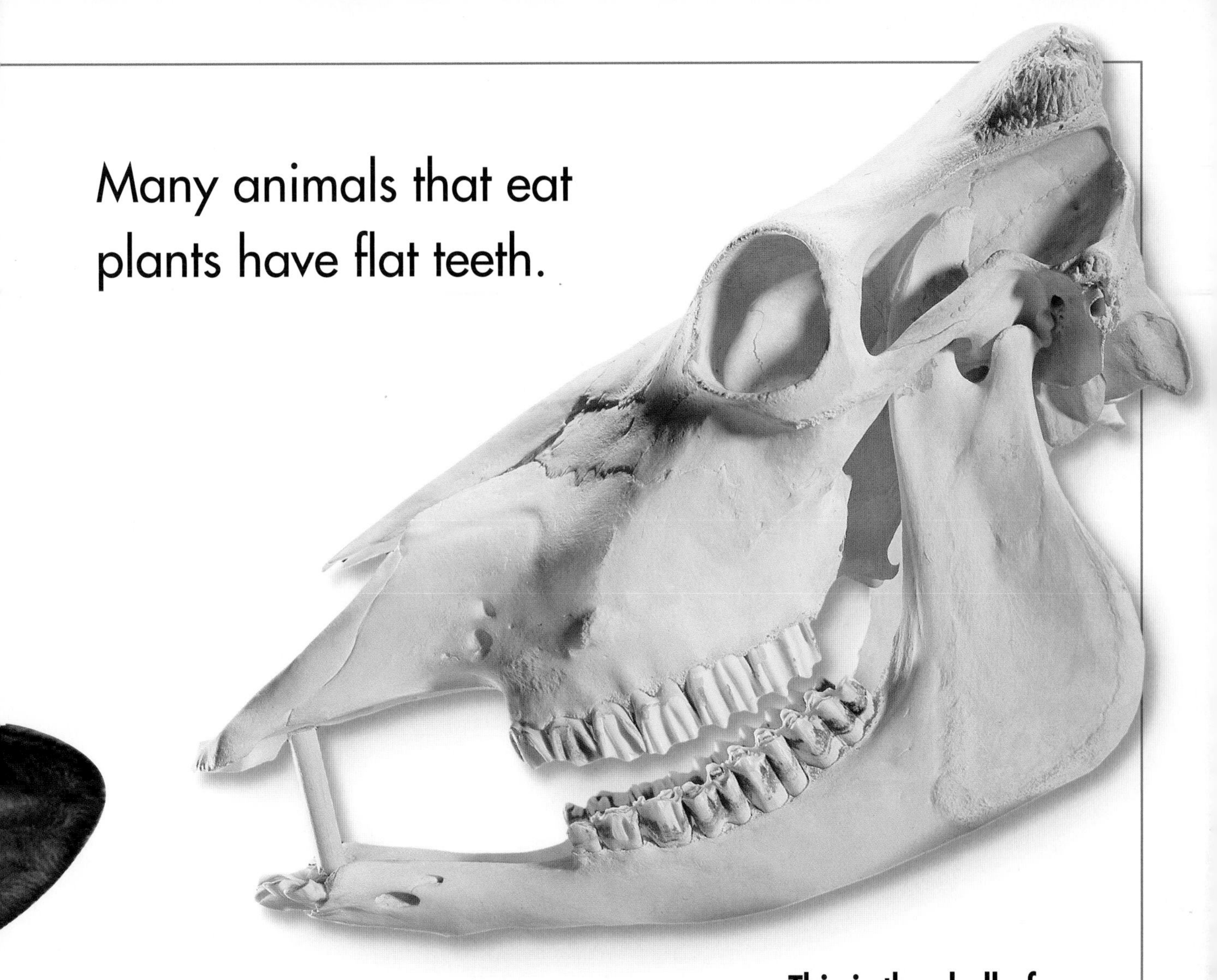

This is the skull of a cow. Look at the flat teeth. Flat teeth help a cow chew plants.

1. What do cows eat for food?

2. How can you tell what cows eat for food?

Grouping Animals

Look at the Venn diagram.
It groups animals by what they eat.

Grouping Animals by What They Eat

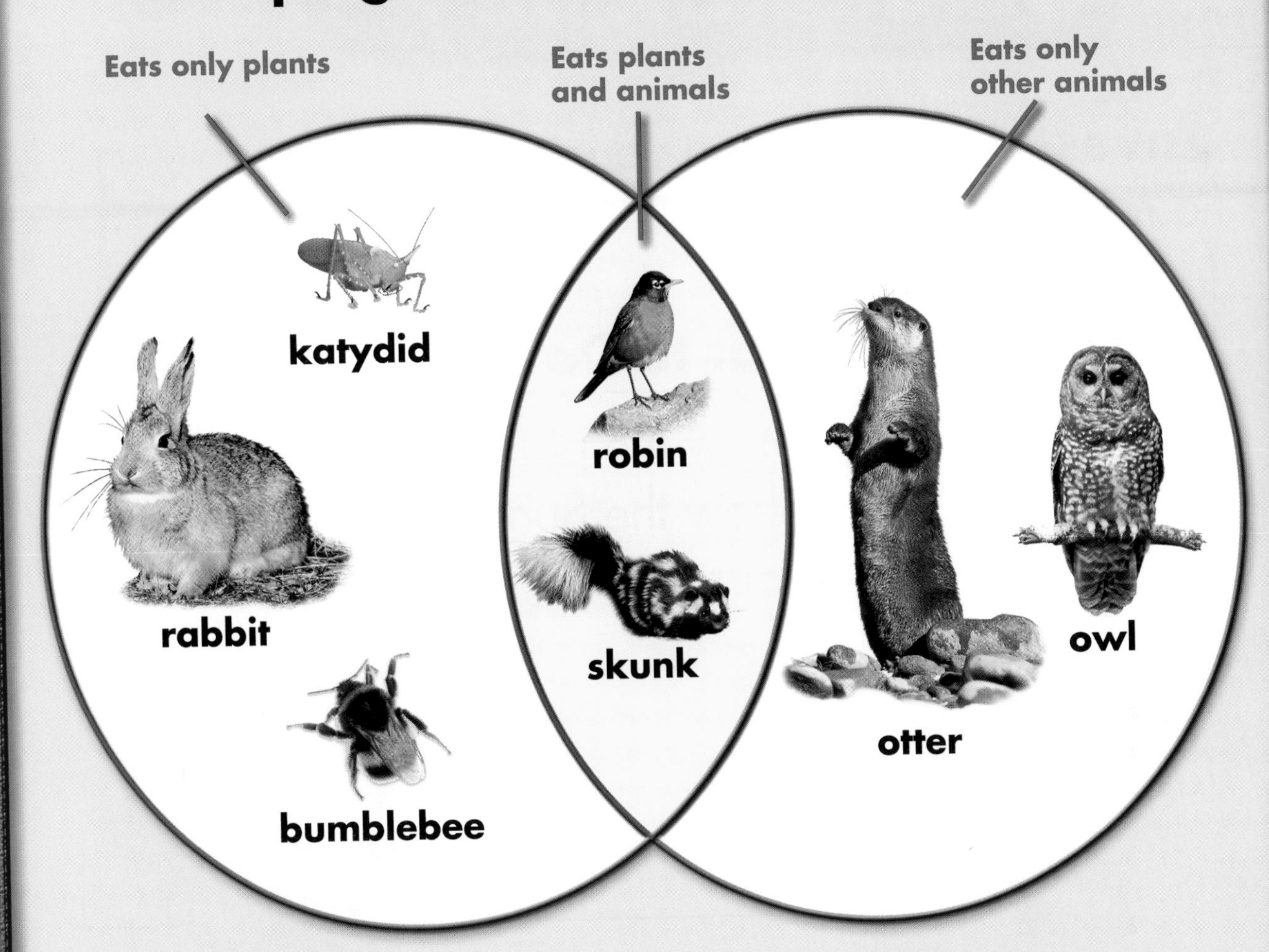

Use the Venn diagram to answer the questions.

1. How many of these animals eat only plants?
2. How many animals eat both plants and animals?
3. How many animals eat only other animals?

Lab zone Take-Home Activity

Find pictures of animals. Work with someone in your family to sort the animals. Make a Venn diagram that shows what the animals eat.

Lab zone Guided Inquiry

Investigate How can you make a model of a food chain?

Materials

paper plates

crayons or markers

masking tape

yarn

What to Do

1. Draw the plant. Show the Sun in your drawing.

2. Draw the rat, snake, and bird from the marsh.

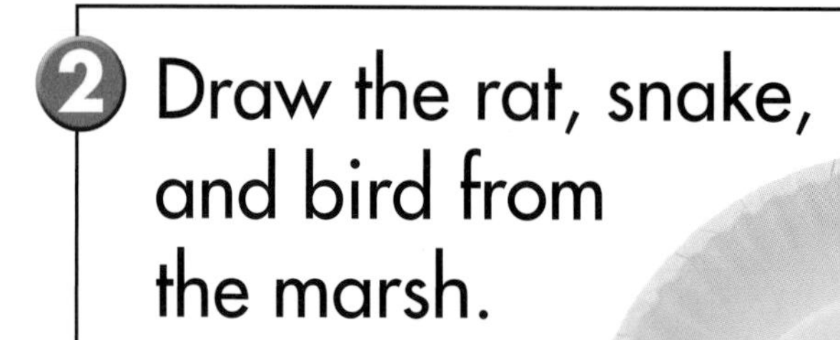

Process Skills

Making a model can help you understand and explain ideas.

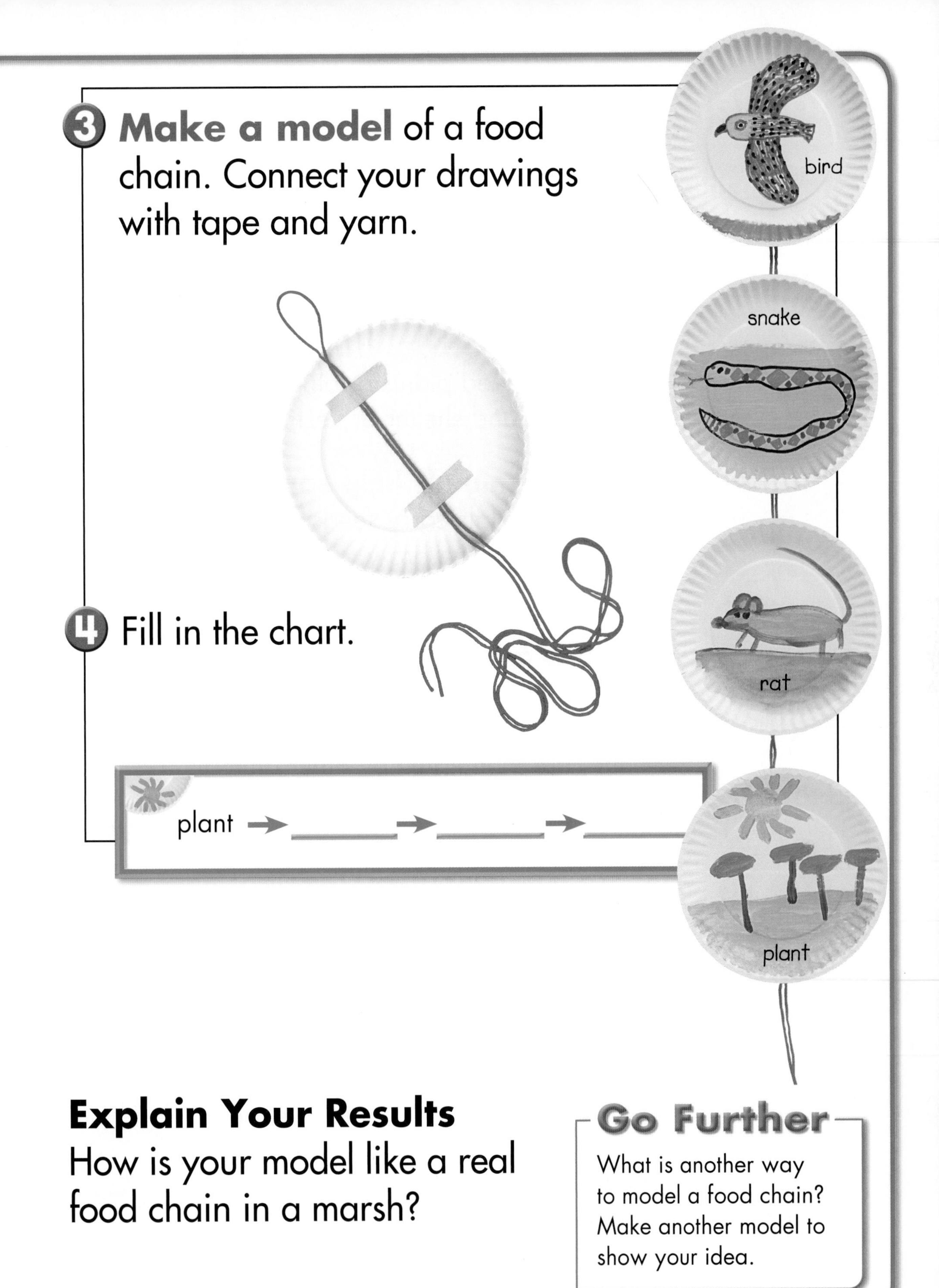

3 **Make a model** of a food chain. Connect your drawings with tape and yarn.

4 Fill in the chart.

plant → ______ → ______ → ______

Explain Your Results

How is your model like a real food chain in a marsh?

Go Further

What is another way to model a food chain? Make another model to show your idea.

Chapter 5 Reviewing Key Concepts

Focus on the BIG Idea Animals eat plants or animals and may use plants or animals for shelter. Some animals may spread seeds of plants.

Lesson 1

How do plants and animals need one another?

- Animals need plants or other animals for food and shelter or nesting.

Lesson 2

How do animals help spread seeds?

- Some animals carry seeds to new places where they can grow.
- Some animals bury seeds and they grow.

Lesson 3

What is a food chain?

- Plants use energy from sunlight to make food, and plants are eaten by animals that are then eaten by other animals.

Lesson 4

How do living things get food in a desert?

- Desert plants and animals depend on each other through food chains.

Lesson 5

How do living things get food in a marsh?

- Marsh plants and animals depend on each other through food chains.

Lesson 6

What do animals eat?

- Animals with sharp, pointed teeth eat other animals for food. Animals with flat teeth eat plants for food.

Cross-Curricular Links

English–Language Arts

Building Vocabulary

Look again at pages 128 and 129. Find the picture for the word **shelter**.

Write a sentence that tells what the wolf cub uses for shelter.

Mathematics

Counting Teeth

Wash your hands and use a mirror to count how many teeth you have.

Write the number that tells how many teeth you have.

History–Social Science

California State Animal

The California grizzly bear is pictured on the California State Flag as a symbol of strength. The grizzly bear has sharp, pointed teeth and smaller flat teeth. What do you infer a grizzly bear eats for food?

Challenge!

Visual and Performing Arts

Food Chain Play

Act out a food chain. Have one person be the Sun. Have other people be plants or animals. Have someone be a human who is at the top of the food chain. Do the play for your class.

Chapter 5 Review/Test

Vocabulary

Which picture goes with each word?

1. shelter (page 134)
2. food chain (page 138)
3. marsh (page 144)

A

B

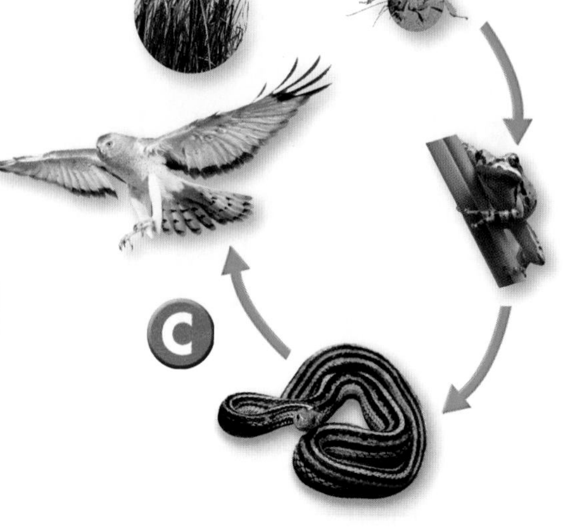
C

Think About It

4. How do animals use plants and other animals? (pages 133–135)
5. What shape are the teeth of animals that eat other animals? (pages 148–149)

6. **Writing in Science** Write a sentence. Tell how squirrels might use trees. (page 134)
7. **Process Skills** **Observe** Look at the skull. What kind of food did this animal eat? (pages 150–151)

8. **Predict** Tell what you think will happen. Read the story to find out. (page 138)

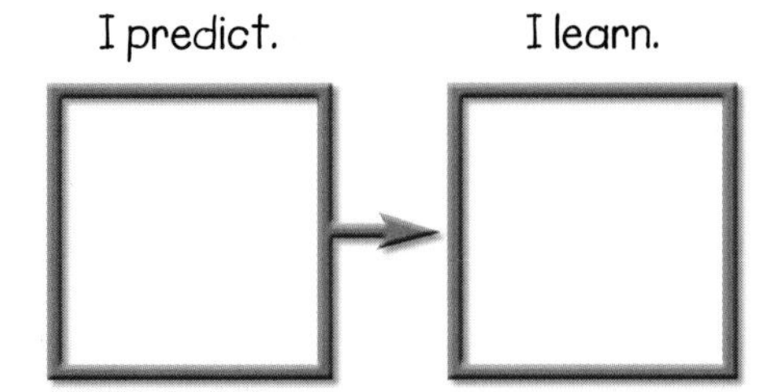

This bear will catch and eat a fish for food.

California Standards Practice

9. Which uses other animals for nesting?

A bird

B wolf

C sea otter

D flea

10. Look at the pictures of the animals. Which does not fit in a marsh food chain?

A roadrunner

B frog

C snake

D hawk

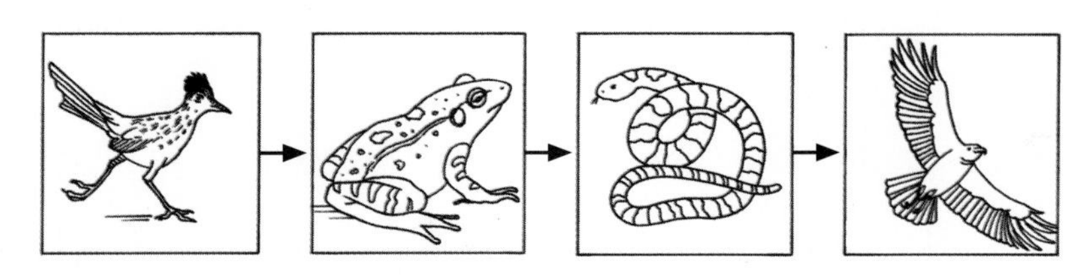

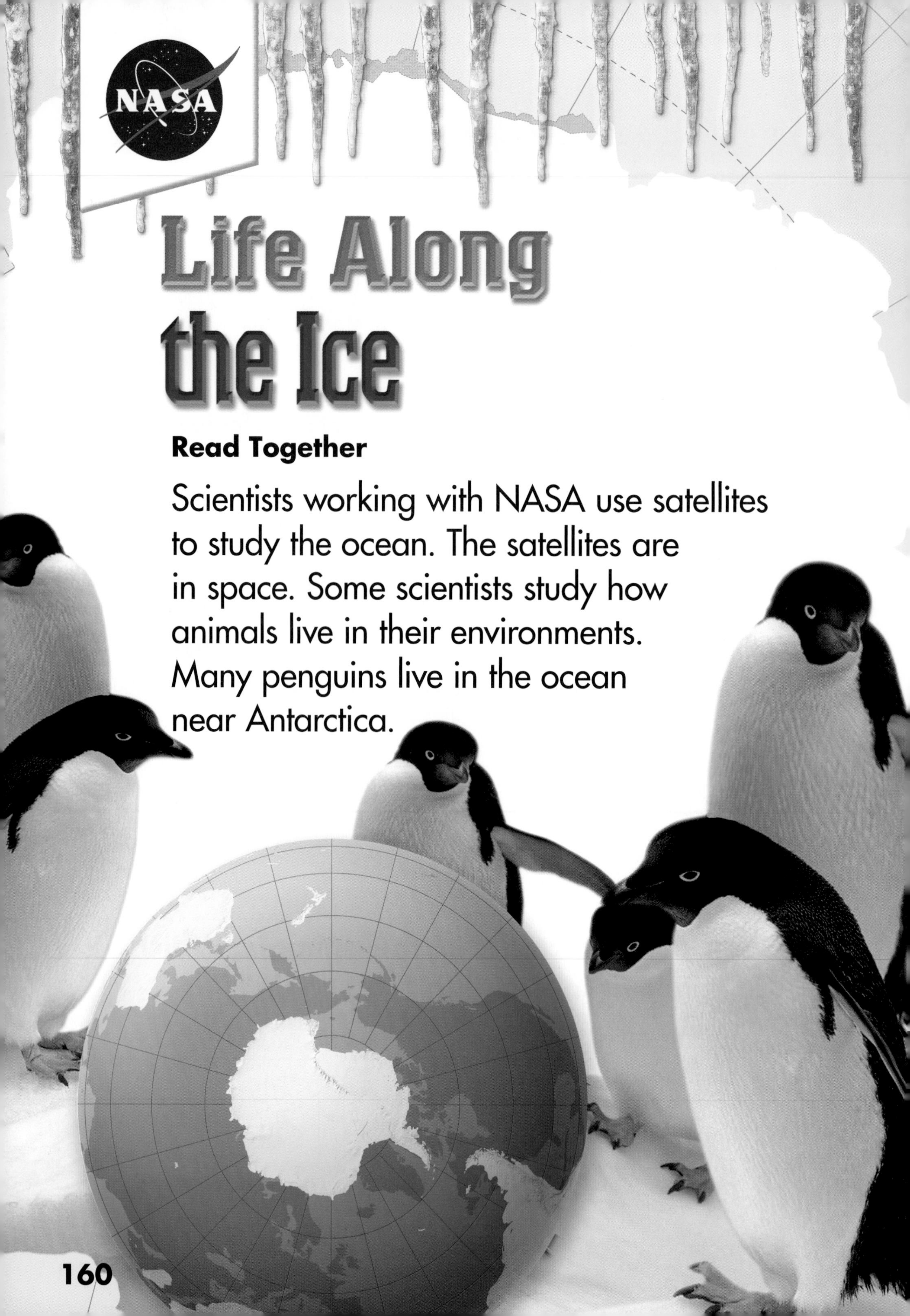

Life Along the Ice

Read Together

Scientists working with NASA use satellites to study the ocean. The satellites are in space. Some scientists study how animals live in their environments. Many penguins live in the ocean near Antarctica.

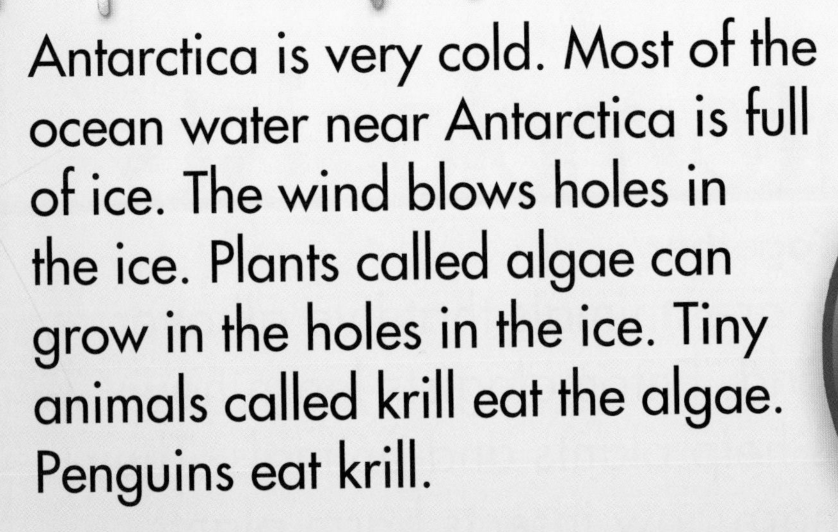

Antarctica is very cold. Most of the ocean water near Antarctica is full of ice. The wind blows holes in the ice. Plants called algae can grow in the holes in the ice. Tiny animals called krill eat the algae. Penguins eat krill.

Krill

The satellites send information about the ocean back to Earth. Scientists have learned that when there are more algae, there are more krill. When there are more krill there are more penguins. When there are fewer krill, there are fewer penguins.

Lab zone **Take-Home Activity**

Draw a picture of a penguin. Tell your family about why krill are important to penguins.

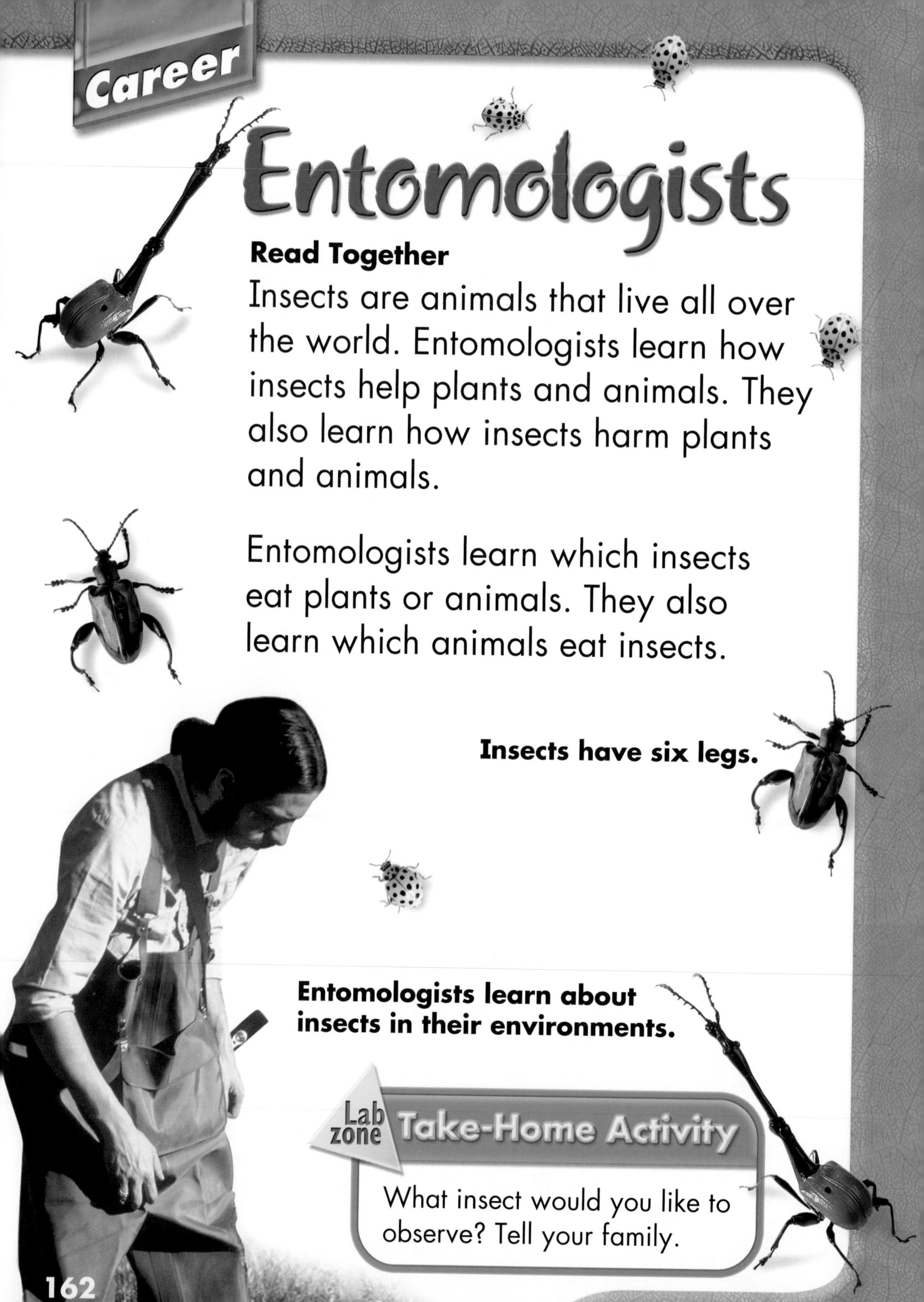

Career

Entomologists

Read Together

Insects are animals that live all over the world. Entomologists learn how insects help plants and animals. They also learn how insects harm plants and animals.

Entomologists learn which insects eat plants or animals. They also learn which animals eat insects.

Insects have six legs.

Entomologists learn about insects in their environments.

Lab zone Take-Home Activity

What insect would you like to observe? Tell your family.

Unit B Summary

Chapter 3

What do plants and animals need?

- Plants need air, water, and energy from light to live.
- Animals need air, water, and food to live.

Chapter 4

Where do plants and animals live?

- Plants and animals live in different environments.
- Plants and animals have parts you can see that help them live in their environments.

Chapter 5

How do plants and animals live together?

- Animals eat plants or other animals for food.
- Animals may help spread seeds and may use plants or other animals for shelter.

Lab zone

Full Inquiry

Experiment How can color help mice stay hidden from hawks?

Use a model. White beans are the field where mice live. Black beans are black mice. Beans with spots are white mice.

Materials

3 bags of beans

paper plate

Ask a question.

How can color help mice stay hidden from hawks?

Make a hypothesis.

Are white beans with spots or black beans easier to see on a white background?

Plan a fair test.

Use the same number of black beans and white beans with spots.

Process Skills

You can do an **experiment** to test a **hypothesis.**

Do your test.

1. One person is the hawk. The hawk must turn away.

2. Put the white beans on the plate. Add 10 black beans and 10 white beans with spots. Mix the beans.

3. Listen for "Go" and "Stop." Let the hawk turn around and pick up mice with one hand.

4. Take turns being the hawk. Record how many beans you pick up.

mice

field

Collect and record data.

Record what you **observe** on a bar graph.

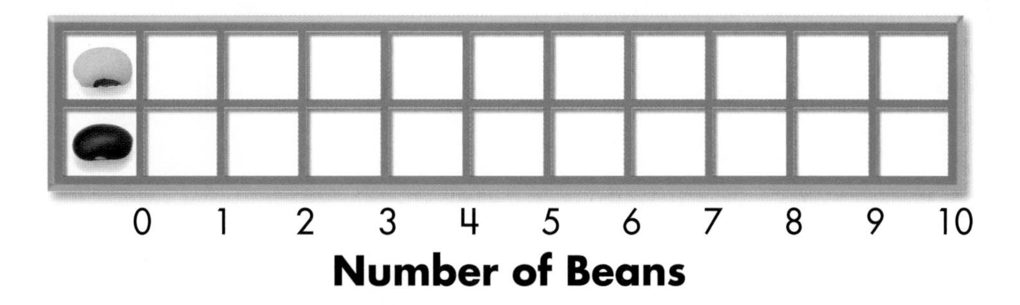

Tell your conclusion.

Which beans were harder to see? Which mice are harder to see in a white environment?

Go Further

What might happen if you added red beans? Do an experiment to find out.

Show What You Know

Make a Model

- Use a shoebox to make a model environment.
- Show plants and animals.
- Show things plants and animals need to live.

Observe Your Teeth

- Try this activity at home. Look at your teeth in a mirror.
- Draw the shapes of different teeth you have. Eat an apple. Observe how you use different teeth as you eat.
- Tell the class what you did and what you observed.

Write a Biography

Talk to an adult who likes to grow plants. Ask that person how he or she grows plants. Write a story about that person and growing plants.

Read More About Life Sciences!

Look for other books about Life Sciences in your library media center. One book you may want to read is:

Biggest, Strongest, Fastest
by Steve Jenkins

This book shows and tells about animals that are the biggest and smallest, fastest and slowest, or strongest and longest.

Science Fair Projects

Full Inquiry

Using Scientific Methods

1. Ask a question.
2. Make a hypothesis.
3. Plan a fair test.
4. Do your test.
5. Record what happens.
6. Tell your conclusions.
7. Go further.

Idea 1

Growing Plants in Soil and Sand

Plan a project.

Find out if plants grow better in soil or sand.

Idea 2

Fresh Water and Salt Water

Plan a project. Find out if plants grow better with fresh water or salt water.

Unit B California Standards Practice

Write the letter of the correct answer.

1. What do plants need to live?

A water, air, and light
B light only
C water only
D animals only

2. What do animals need to live?

A food only
B water only
C light only
D water, air, and food

California Field Trip

The Exploratorium

San Francisco, California

The Exploratorium is a museum in San Francisco. You can pump air into a machine to make fog. You can start a dust storm. You can even make a tornado!

San Francisco

Find Out More

Research to find out more about different kinds of weather.

- Draw a picture that shows a kind of weather.
- Write a sentence that tells about your picture.

- What is weather?
- How hot or cold is the weather?
- How can you measure rain?
- What does the Sun do?

Chapter 6

Observing Weather

DIGITAL SE

Focus on the BIG Idea

How can you tell about the weather?

weather

wind vane

thermometer

temperature

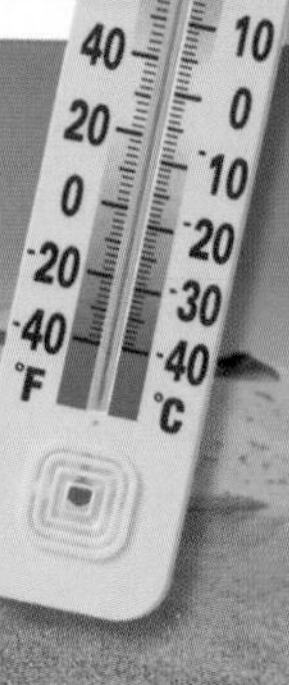

Chapter 6 Vocabulary

weather page 181

wind vane page 183

temperature page 184

thermometer page 185

rain gauge page 187

Lab zone Directed Inquiry

Explore What does a wind vane measure?

Materials

paper plate

marker

clay

straw

tissue strip

masking tape

What to Do

1. Label the plate. Add clay.
2. Tape the tissue to the straw. Put it in the clay.
3. **Observe** outside.

Process Skills

You can **communicate** by answering questions.

Explain Your Results

Communicate Compare your results with others. **Observe** again if they are not the same.

How to Read Science

Reading Skills

Ask and Answer Questions

The words *who, what, when, where,* or *how* start a question. You can answer questions about what you read.

Science Story

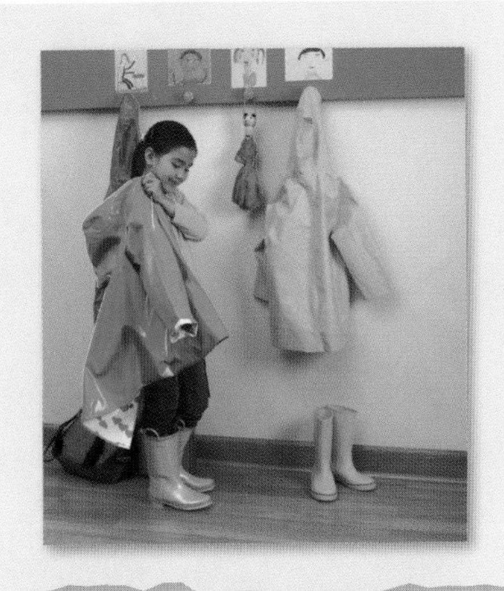

Weather can change from day to day. The girl is going outside. The girl is putting on a raincoat.

Apply It!

Communicate

Where is the girl going?

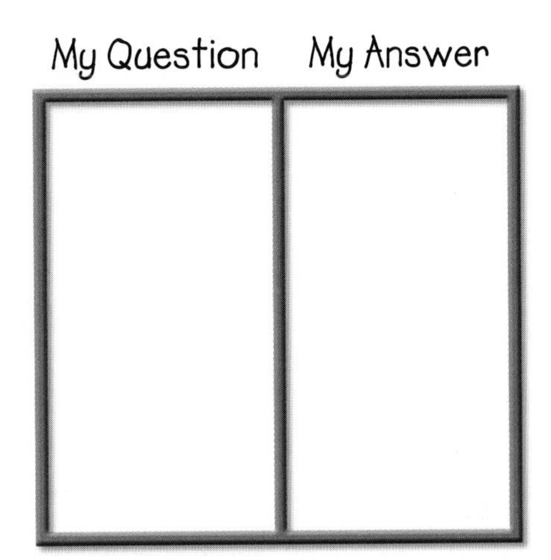

You Are There

All Kinds of Weather

Sung to the tune of "Yankee Doodle"
Lyrics by Gerri Brioso & Richard Freitas/The Dovetail Group, Inc.

There's all kinds of weather and
Of that I'm really sure.
Just open up a window
Or peek out an open door.

Lesson 1

What is weather?

Weather changes from day to day. **Weather** is what it is like outside. Weather may be windy or still. Weather may be wet or dry. Weather may be hot or cold too.

You will learn how weather changes from season to season in Chapter 7.

A windy day is great for flying a kite!

DIGITAL NSTA SciLinks keyword: weather code: gr1p181

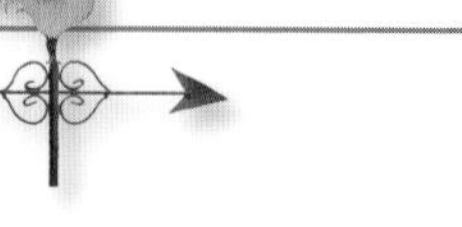

Windy Weather

Wind is moving air.
Look at the trees in the picture.
How can you tell which way
the wind is blowing?

You can use a weather tool.
The weather tool is a wind vane.
A **wind vane** points into the wind.

Look at the wind vane.
The arrow points to where the wind is coming from.

Lesson Review

1. What is weather?

2. **Ask and Answer Questions**
   What does a wind vane show you?

Lesson 2

How hot or cold is the weather?

You know weather can be hot or cold.

Temperature is how hot or cold something is.

You can measure temperature.

You can measure the temperature of weather.

Look at the boys run. Why do you think they are wearing jackets?

A **thermometer** is a tool that measures temperature.
The numbers show the temperature.
The red line goes up as the air gets warmer.
The red line goes down as the air gets cooler.

1. What is temperature?

2. **Ask and Answer Questions** How does a thermometer show the temperature?

Lesson 3

How can you measure rain?

Pitter-patter! It is starting to rain. Rain is water that falls from clouds. Rain falls in drops.

How can you tell how much rain falls?

You can use a weather tool.
A **rain gauge** is a tool
to measure the amount of rain.
A rain gauge is open on top.
Rain falls into the rain gauge.
The numbers show how
much rain falls.

Look at how much rain has fallen.

1. What is a rain gauge?
2. **Writing in Science** Describe how a rain gauge works.

Look for Active Art animations at www.pearsonsuccessnet.com

Lesson 4

What does the Sun do?

Think of a bright sunny day.
How does the light from the Sun feel on your skin?

Today is cloudy. You cannot see the Sun. The playground stays cool all day.

It is noon. The Sun is shining brightly. The playground was cool this morning. Now it is hot!

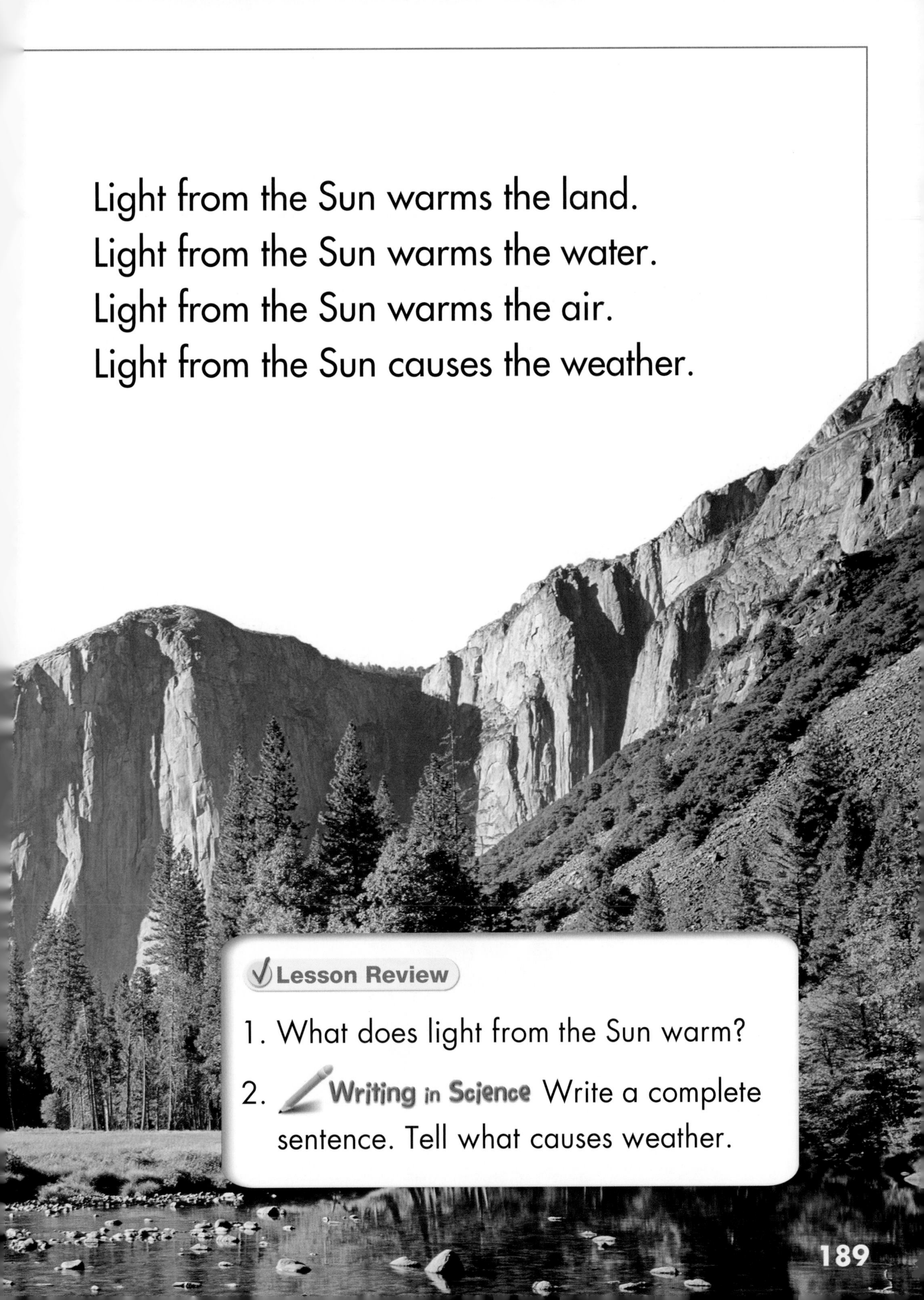

Light from the Sun warms the land.
Light from the Sun warms the water.
Light from the Sun warms the air.
Light from the Sun causes the weather.

Lesson Review

1. What does light from the Sun warm?
2. **Writing in Science** Write a complete sentence. Tell what causes weather.

Math in Science

Using a Bar Graph

Map Facts

San Francisco, California, usually gets about 52 cm of rain each year.

DIGITAL

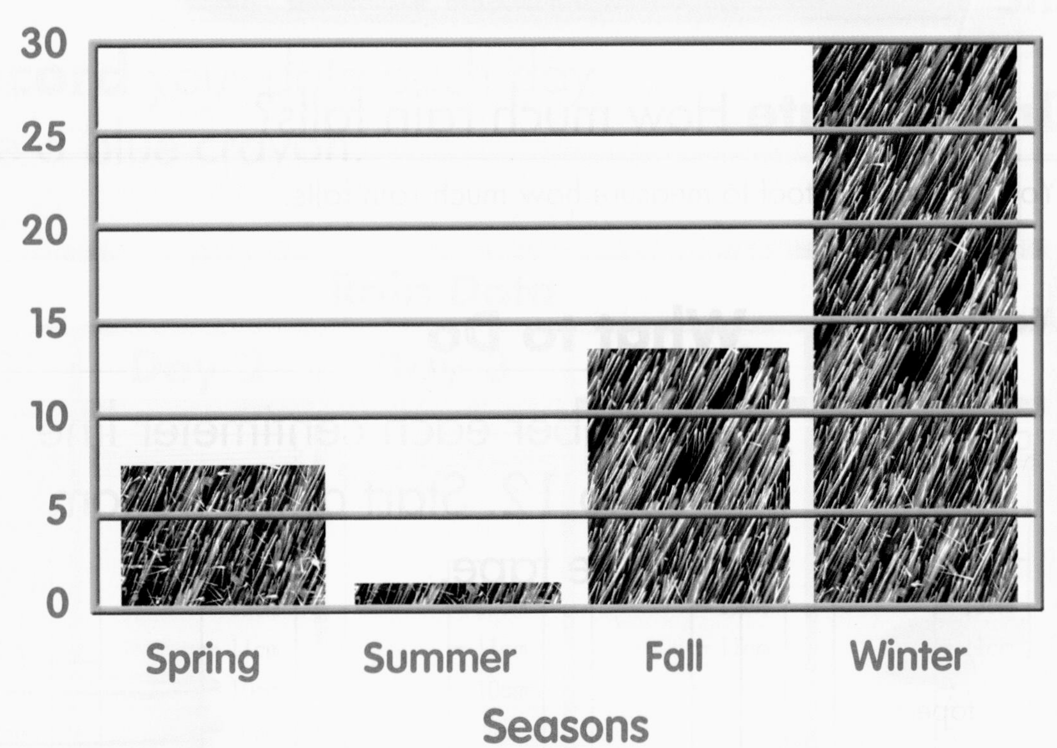

Use the bar graph to answer these questions.

1. Which season gets the most rain in San Francisco, California?
2. Which season gets the least rain in San Francisco, California?

Lab zone Take-Home Activity

Compare the amount of rain in spring and fall. Does San Francisco usually get more rain in spring or in fall? Tell your family.

Read Together

Many satellites move around Earth. NASA scientists send satellites into space. Satellites take pictures of Earth. Satellite pictures help scientists study weather. Satellite pictures show how well crops are growing. Satellite pictures can spot forest fires too.

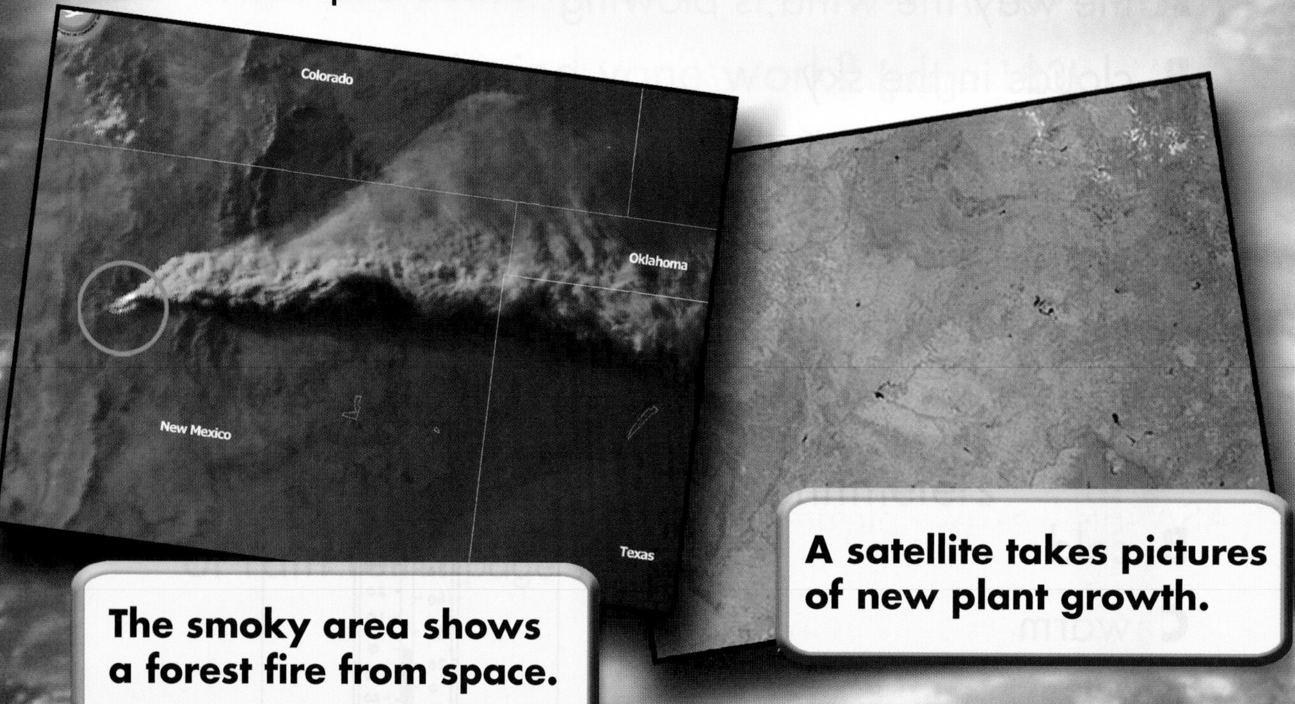

The smoky area shows a forest fire from space.

A satellite takes pictures of new plant growth.

Lab zone Take-Home Activity

NASA satellites take pictures of Earth. Draw a picture of a satellite to show your family. Tell your family how satellites can help scientists learn about weather on Earth.

Meteorologist

Read Together

Dr. J. Marshall Shepherd is a meteorologist at NASA.

A meteorologist is a scientist who studies or predicts the weather. First, some meteorologists use special weather tools to collect data.

Next, some meteorologists make special maps about the weather.

Last, some meteorologists share their predictions about what the weather will be like.

Dr. Shepherd does science experiments. The experiments help us to better understand Earth and its weather.

Lab zone Take-Home Activity

Look at a weather map in a newspaper. Find out what the weather might be like tomorrow.

CALIFORNIA Standards Focus Questions

- What is a season?
- What is weather like in summer?
- What is weather like in fall?
- What is weather like in winter?

Chapter 7

Seasons

Focus on the BIG Idea

What is the weather like in different seasons?

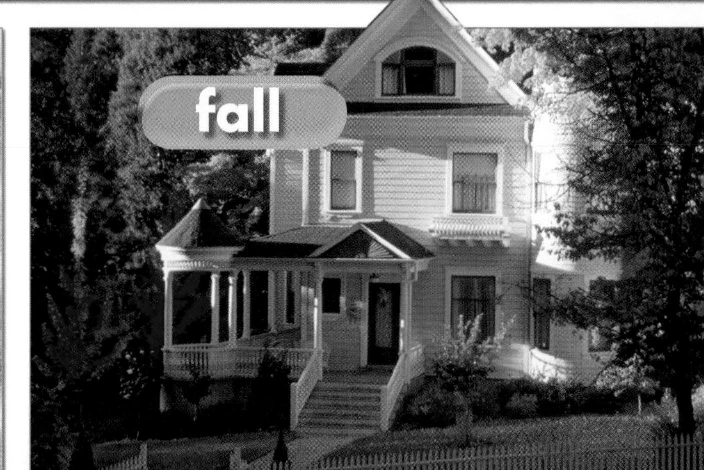

DIGITAL

Chapter 7
Vocabulary
season page 207
spring page 208
summer page 210
fall page 212
winter page 214
winter

Lab zone

Directed Inquiry

Explore What is the weather like in different seasons?

Materials

paper

crayons

What to Do

1. **Observe** the weather. Write the season.
2. Draw yourself outside. Show what you would wear.

3. Make drawings for the other seasons.

Process Skills

When you **communicate** you share what you know.

Explain Your Results

Communicate Tell how the weather changes from season to season.

How to Read Science

Retell

Retell means to tell what you learned in your own words.

Science Story

Beth and Hugo live on a mountain. Winter is their favorite season. It snows a lot in the winter. Beth and Hugo like to go sledding in the snow.

Apply It!

Communicate Tell why Beth and Hugo like winter.

Retell

You Are There

Can I Go Outside and Play?

Sung to the tune of "Oh Susannah"
Lyrics by Gerri Brioso & Richard Freitas/The Dovetail Group, Inc.

In winter it gets very cold,
And sometimes there is snow.
I need to wear a hat and gloves,
And then I'm ready to go!

Lesson 1

What is a season?

You know weather changes from day to day.
Weather changes from season to season too.

A **season** is a time of year.
You can predict the weather for each season.
A season may be warm or cold.
A season may be wet or dry.

Look at the snow! What season do you think it is?

DIGITAL NSTA SciLinks keyword: season code: gr1p207

Weather in Spring

Spring is one of the four seasons.
Spring comes after winter.
You can predict what weather
will be like in spring.

Warm weather and rain help spring flowers grow.

A mother sea lion and her cub play in the warm spring air.

Temperatures get warmer in spring.
Some spring days are rainy.
Spring has more daylight
than winter.
Spring weather can be different
in different places.

1. What is a season?

2. **Retell** Tell what you learned about weather in spring.

Lesson 2

What is the weather like in summer?

Summer is one of the four seasons. **Summer** comes after spring. You can predict what weather will be like in summer.

It may rain very little in summer. Plants need to be watered.

Summer nights can be cool and foggy in some places. Fog is a cloud near the ground.

Summer is the warmest season.
Summer may be very dry.
Some places get very little rain.
Summer weather can be different in different places.

1. What is summer?

2. **Retell** Tell what you learned about weather in summer.

Lesson 3

What is the weather like in fall?

Fall is one of the four seasons.
Fall comes after summer.
You can predict what weather will be like in fall.

The Sun sets earlier in fall than in summer.

Some trees change colors when days get cooler in fall.

Fall is cooler than summer.
Some fall days are rainy.
Fall has less daylight than summer.
Fall weather can be different in different places.

Lesson Review

1. What is fall?
2. **Writing in Science** Describe what fall weather is like.

Math in Science

Charting Favorite Seasons

Nan asked her classmates what their favorite season was. Nan made a chart to show what they said.

Favorite Season

Spring	3 figures
Summer	10 figures
Fall	5 figures
Winter	8 figures

1. How many children like summer best?
2. Which season is the favorite of the least number of children?
3. How many more children like fall best than like spring best?

Lab zone Take-Home Activity

Ask friends or family members what their favorite season is. Make a chart like Nan made. Which season is liked best?

Lab zone

Guided Inquiry

Investigate How does the temperature change from day to day?

Materials

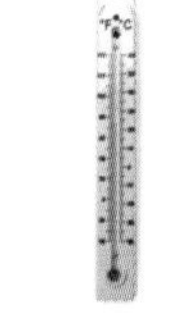

thermometer

red crayons

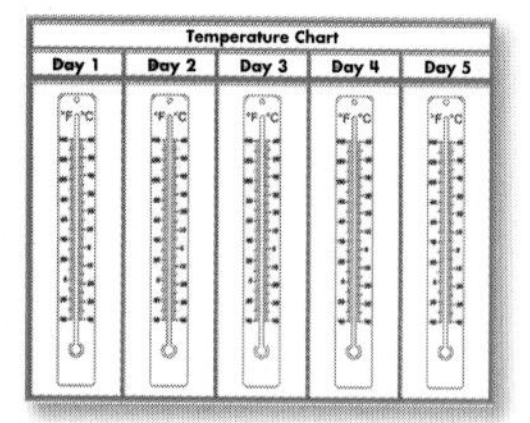

Temperature Chart

What to Do

1 **Measure** the temperature outside at the same time each day.

2 Record the temperature each day. Use a red crayon.

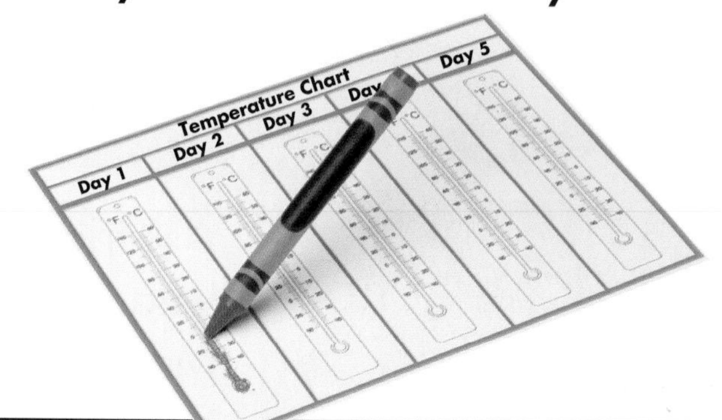

Process Skills

You can use a thermometer to **measure** temperature.

DIGITAL Lab zone

3 Compare the temperatures.

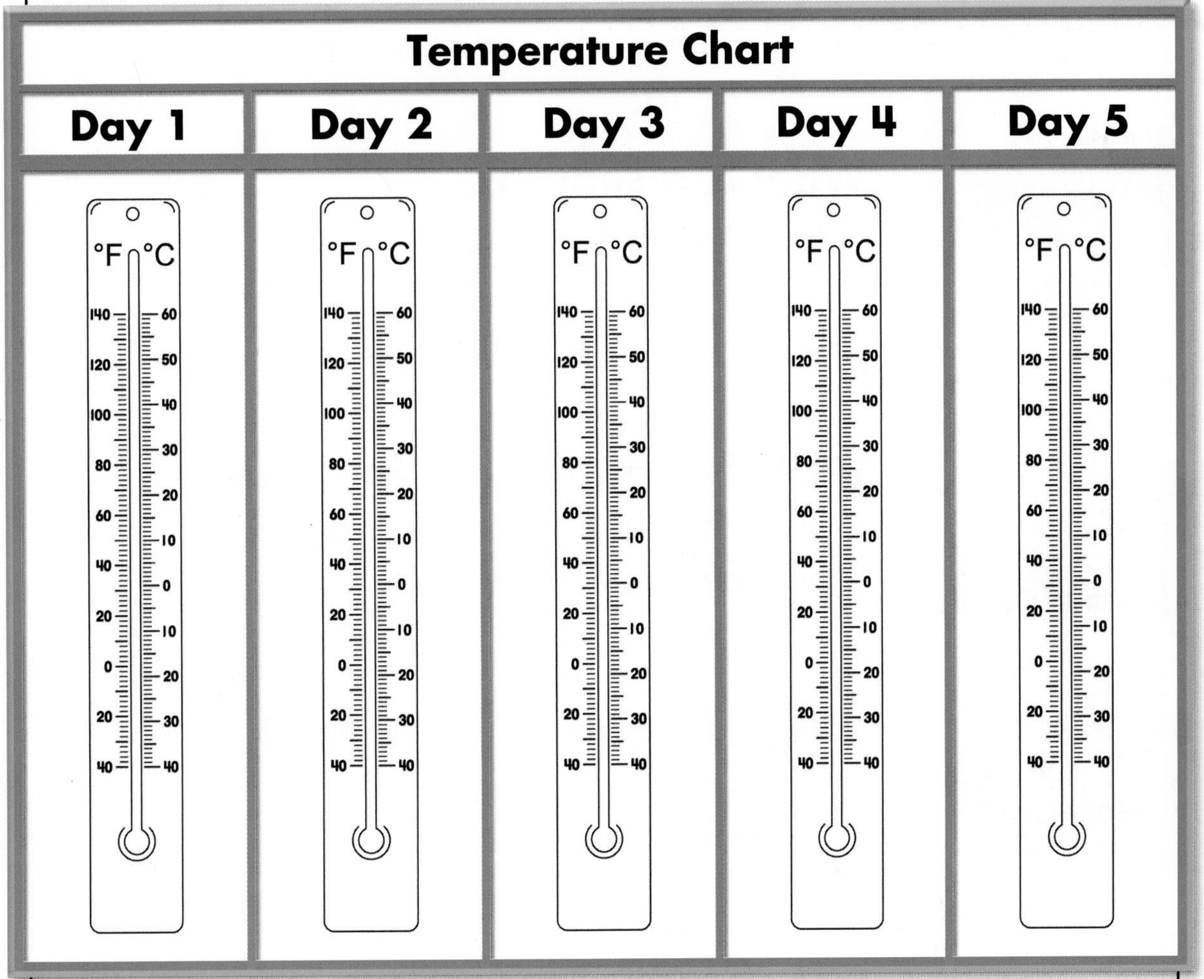

Temperature Chart				
Day 1	Day 2	Day 3	Day 4	Day 5
°F °C	°F °C	°F °C	°F °C	°F °C
140 60	140 60	140 60	140 60	140 60
50	50	50	50	50
120 40	120 40	120 40	120 40	120 40
100 30	100 30	100 30	100 30	100 30
80 20	80 20	80 20	80 20	80 20
60 10	60 10	60 10	60 10	60 10
40 0	40 0	40 0	40 0	40 0
20 10	20 10	20 10	20 10	20 10
0 20	0 20	0 20	0 20	0 20
20 30	20 30	20 30	20 30	20 30
40 40	40 40	40 40	40 40	40 40

Explain Your Results

What did you use to **measure** the temperature? How did the temperature change?

Go Further

How does the temperature change from season to season where you live? Make a plan to find out.

Chapter 7 Reviewing Key Concepts

Focus on the BIG Idea

Spring, summer, winter, and fall are four seasons. You can predict what weather will be like in a season.

Lesson 1

What is a season?

- A season is a time of year.
- You can predict what weather will be like in a season.

Lesson 2

What is weather like in summer?

- Summer is the warmest season.
- Summer may be very dry.

Lesson 3

What is weather like in fall?

- Fall is cooler than summer.
- Some fall days are rainy.

Lesson 4

What is weather like in winter?

- Winter is the coldest season.
- Winter may be the wettest season too.

Cross-Curricular Links

English–Language Arts

Building Vocabulary

Look again at pages 202 and 203. Find the pictures for the words **spring** and **winter**.

Write a sentence that tells how weather in spring is different from weather in winter.

Mathematics

Comparing Rainfall

A town gets about 5 centimeters of rain in the spring. This town gets about 10 centimeters of rain in the fall.

How much more rain does the town get in the fall than it gets in the spring?

Visual and Performing Arts

Describing Tree Patterns

Look again at page 216. Find the pictures of the tree in spring, summer, fall, and winter.

Describe how the tree changes. Draw and color your own picture of a tree in each season.

Challenge!

Mathematics

Making a Bar Graph

Work with an adult. Find an Internet site that shows how much rain usually falls each month where you live. Make a bar graph that compares the month that gets the most rain with the month that gets the least rain.

Chapter 7 Review/Test

Vocabulary

Which picture goes with each word?

1. spring (page 208)
2. summer (page 210)
3. fall (page 212)
4. winter (page 214)

A

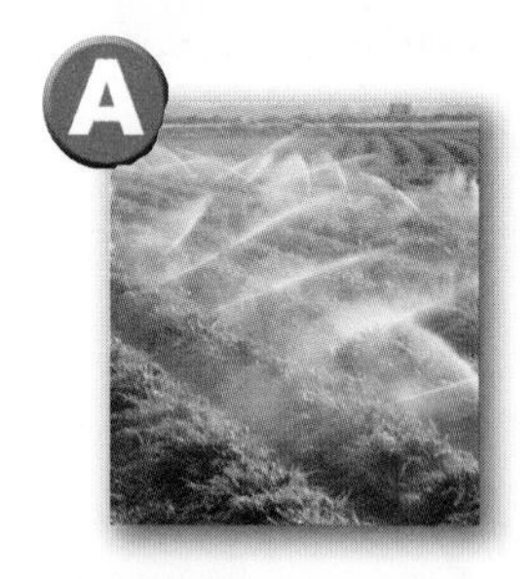

B

C

D

Think About It

5. Which season is the coldest and may be the wettest? (pages 214–215)
6. Which season is the warmest and may be very dry? (pages 210–211)

7. **Writing in Science** Write two sentences. Tell what fall weather is like. (pages 212–213)

8. **Process Skills** **Communicate** What is spring weather like where you live? (pages 208–209)

9. **Retell** Tell what you learned about weather in a season. (page 207)

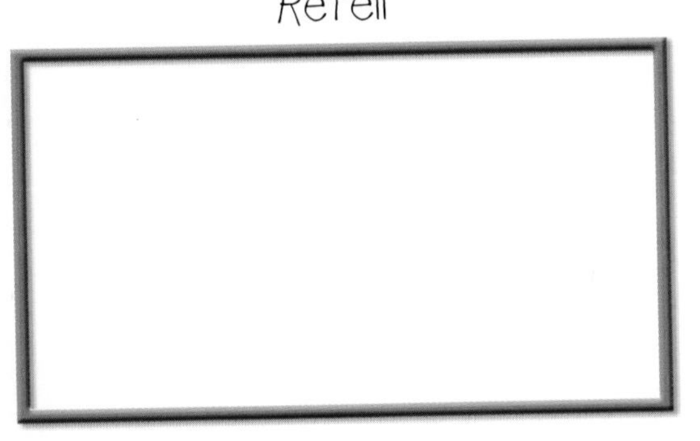

You can predict what temperatures will be like in a season. You can predict how much rain will fall in a season too.

California Standards Practice

Write the letter of the correct answer.

10. Which answer tells what a season is?

A a time of year

B a time of day

C a day of the week

D a part of the ocean

11. Look at the bar graph. Which season has the most rainfall?

A spring

B summer

C fall

D winter

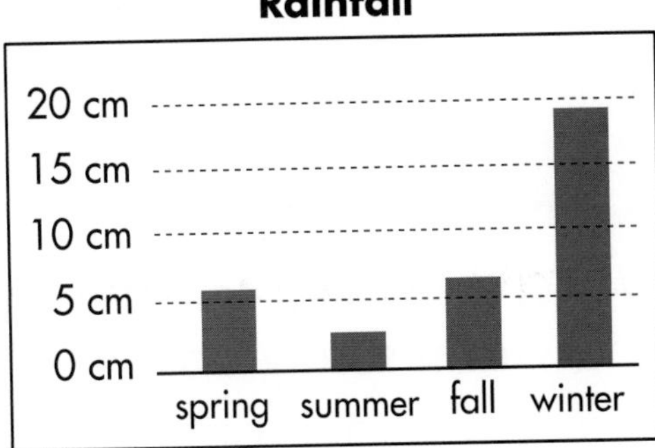

Career

Farmer

Read Together

Farmers have an important job to do! Farmers care for plants and animals. People depend on farmers for food.

Different places have different growing seasons. Some farmers grow strawberries. Strawberries are a fruit. Strawberries grow best on warm sunny days and cool foggy nights.

Farmers can grow strawberries all year in southern California. *Yum!*

Lab zone **Take-Home Activity**

Draw a picture of a farm on a warm sunny day. Tell your family about farmers.

Unit C Summary

Chapter 6

How can you tell about the weather?

- Weather is what it is like outside.
- Weather changes from day to day.
- Weather can be measured using a thermometer, wind vane, and rain gauge.

Chapter 7

What is the weather like in different seasons?

- Spring weather gets warmer and may have rainy days.
- Summer is the warmest season and may be very dry.
- Fall weather gets cooler and may have rainy days.
- Winter is the coldest season and may have the most rain or snow.

Lab zone Full Inquiry

Experiment Does the Sun warm land or water faster?

The sunlight warms Earth's land and water during the day. Does the sunlight warm land and water in the same way?

Materials

cup with water and cup with soil

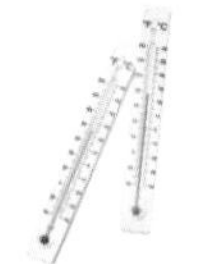

2 thermometers

lamp

Ask a question.

Does sunlight warm the land or water faster?

Make a hypothesis.

Will a cup of soil warm faster than a cup of water? Tell what you think.

Plan a fair test.

Make sure the lamp is placed evenly above both cups.

Do your test.

1 Put one thermometer in the soil. Put the other thermometer in the water.

The soil is like land.

Process Skills

You plan a **fair test** in an experiment when you choose the one thing that you will change.

2. Wait for 30 minutes. Record the temperatures.

3. Place the lamp so the light shines on both cups.

4. Wait 1 hour. **Observe.** Record.

5. Turn the light off.

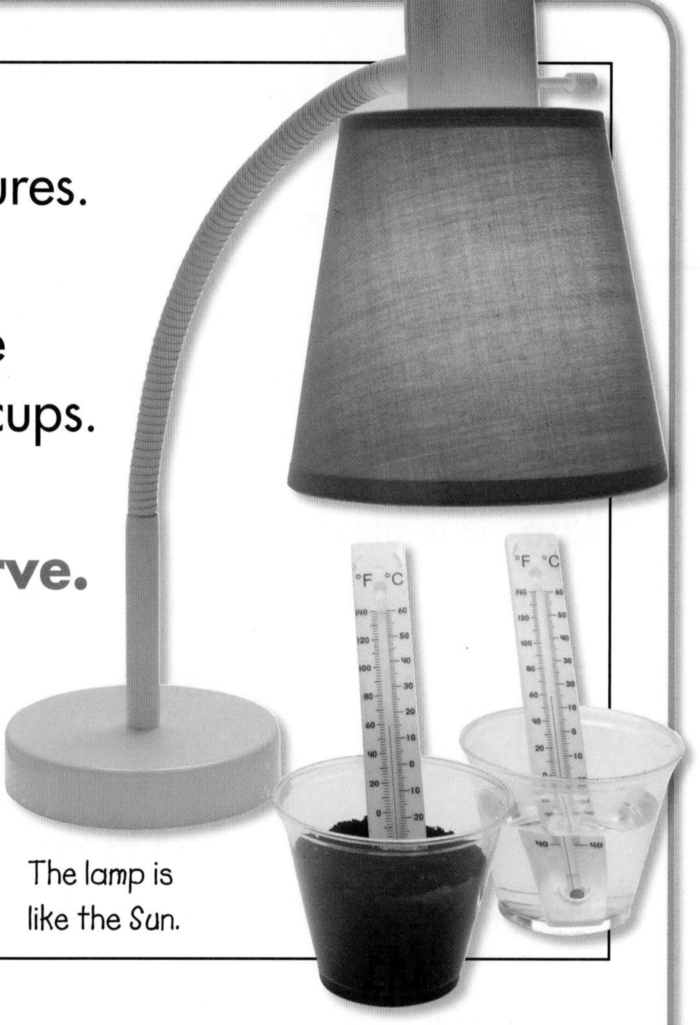

The lamp is like the Sun.

Collect and record data.

	Temperature at start	Temperature after 1 hour
Soil	_____ °C	_____ °C
Water	_____ °C	_____ °C

Tell your conclusion.

Did soil or water warm faster? Do you think the Sun warms land or water faster? Why?

Go Further

What might happen if you used bright sunlight instead of a lamp? Try it and find out.

Show What You Know

Make a Poster

- Draw or cut out pictures from a magazine showing the four seasons.
- Use your pictures to make a poster.
- Tell about the weather in each season.

Make a Weather Calendar

- Make a weather calendar for 1 week. Draw a picture of the weather for each day. Show if it is sunny, cloudy, or rainy. Write words that describe the weather each day.

Write a Play

- Write a play about your favorite season. Write parts that your classmates can say and act out.

Read More About Earth Sciences

Look for other books about Earth Sciences in your library media center. One book you may want to read is:

Cloud Dance
by Thomas Locker

This book has great pictures and tells about different kinds of clouds.

Discovery Channel School

Science Fair Projects

Full Inquiry

Using Scientific Methods
1. Ask a question.
2. Make a hypothesis.
3. Plan a fair test.
4. Do your test.
5. Record what happens.
6. Tell your conclusions.
7. Go further.

Idea 1

Measuring Temperature

Plan a project. Find out how air temperature outside changes during the day.

Idea 2

Comparing Temperature

Plan a project. Find out if predicted temperatures are the same as actual temperatures.

Write the letter of the correct answer.

1. Which tool is used to measure weather?

A pan balance

B measuring cup

C ruler

D rain gauge

2. Look at the picture. What is the temperature outside like?

A cold

B rainy

C hot

D windy

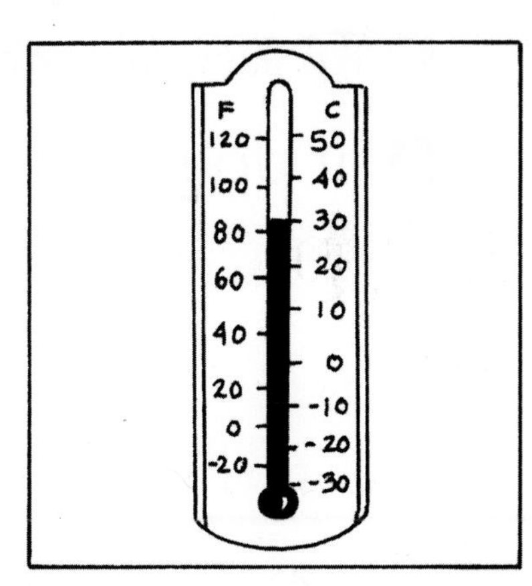

3. Which answer tells about a wind vane?

A It measures the temperature.

B It measures rainfall.

C It measures weight.

D It shows which way the wind is blowing.

4. What tells about the Sun?

A It does not cause weather.

B It is cool.

C It warms the air, land, and water.

D It does not warm people.

5. What will the playground be like on a cloudy day?

A It will stay hot all day.

B It will be warm in the morning and cool in the afternoon.

C It will stay cool all day.

D It will be cool in the morning and hot in the afternoon.

6. Which one is a season?

A March

B fall

C temperature

D Sun

California Science Content Standards, Grade 1

STANDARD SET 2. Life Sciences	
1LS2.0 Plants and animals meet their needs in different ways. As a basis for understanding this concept:	
1LS2.a *Students know* different plants and animals inhabit different kinds of environments and have external features that help them thrive in different kinds of places.	pp. 100, 102, **103, 104,** 105, 106, 107, 108, 109, **110,** 111, 112, 113, 114, 115, 116, 117, 120, 121, **122, 124, 125,** 144, 145, 160, 161, **163,** 164, 165, 166, **170, 171**
1LS2.b *Students know* both plants and animals need water; animals need food, and plants need light.	pp. **76, 78,** 79, **80,** 81, **87, 90, 91, 92, 94,** 138, **163, 169**
1LS2.c *Students know* animals eat plants or other animals for food and may also use plants or even other animals for shelter and nesting.	pp. 130, 132, **133, 134,** 135, **138,** 139, 140, 141, 142, 143, 144, 145, 146, 147, 148, 150, 154, 155, **156,** 158, 159, **163,** 164, 165, **171, 172**
1LS2.d *Students know* how to infer what animals eat from the shapes of their teeth (e.g., sharp teeth: eats meat; flat teeth: eats plants).	pp. 148, **149, 150, 151, 156, 158, 172**
1LS2.e *Students know* roots are associated with the intake of water and soil nutrients and green leaves are associated with making food from sunlight.	pp. 82, **83, 84, 85,** 90, 91, **92, 94, 95**

What It Means to You

You know that different plants and animals live together in different places. You know that plants have different parts and animals have different body parts that help them live in their environment.

You know what plants and animals need to live. You know that plants make food and animals eat food. You know that plants and animals depend on each other for food or shelter. You can infer what some animals eat by looking at their teeth.

California Science Content Standards, Grade 1

STANDARD SET 3. Earth Sciences	
1ES3.0 Weather can be observed, measured, and described. As a basis for understanding this concept:	
1ES3.a *Students know* how to use simple tools (e.g., thermometer, wind vane) to measure weather conditions and record changes from day to day and across the seasons.	pp. **178, 183,** 184, **185,** 186, **187, 192, 193, 194, 196, 197,** 218, 219, **225, 226, 231, 232**
1ES3.b *Students know* that the weather changes from day to day but trends in temperature or rain (or snow) tend to be predictable during a season.	pp. 180, **181, 184, 194, 196, 197,** 204, 206, **207,** 208, 209, 210, 211, 212, 213, 214, 215, 218, 219, **220, 222, 223, 225,** 228, **233, 234**
1ES3.c *Students know* the sun warms the land, air, and water.	pp. 188, **189, 194, 196, 197, 226, 227, 232**

What It Means to You

You can use a wind vane, a thermometer, or a rain gauge to tell about weather. You know weather changes from day to day. You know how to keep records of weather changes.

You know what weather is like in different seasons. You can predict what the weather will be like in each season. You know that the Sun warms the land, air, and water all around you.

STANDARD SET 4. Investigation and Experimentation

1IE4.0 Scientific progress is made by asking meaningful questions and conducting careful investigations. As a basis for understanding this concept and addressing the content in the other three strands, students should develop their own questions and perform investigations. Students will:

1IE4.a Draw pictures that portray some features of the thing being described.	pp. **63, 100, 120, 121, 154, 155, 204**
1IE4.b Record observations and data with pictures, numbers, or written statements.	pp. **6, 24, 25, 36, 54, 55, 63,** 76, **91, 120, 121, 130, 154, 155, 192, 193,** 204, **218, 219, 227**
1IE4.c Record observations on a bar graph.	pp. **52, 53, 165**
1IE4.d Describe the relative position of objects by using two references (e.g., above and next to, below and left of).	pp. **22, 23, 57**
1IE4.e Make new observations when discrepancies exist between two descriptions of the same object or phenomenon.	pp. **178**

What It Means to You

Investigations help you answer questions. You use pictures or words to tell what you see. You can use the numbers to tell temperature and amount. You can use a bar graph to show what you learn. You can see if your results are alike those of other children in your class. You can observe again if your results are not the same. You can tell where things are by looking at the objects around them.

Glossary

The glossary uses letters and signs to show how words are pronounced. The mark ′ is placed after a syllable with a primary or heavy accent. The mark ′ is placed after a syllable with a secondary or lighter accent.

To hear these words pronounced, listen to the AudioText CD.

Pronunciation Key

a	in hat	ō	in open	sh	in she
ā	in age	ȯ	in all	th	in thin
â	in care	ô	in order	ᴛʜ	in then
ä	in far	oi	in oil	zh	in measure
e	in let	ou	in out	ə	= a in about
ē	in equal	u	in cup	ə	= e in taken
ėr	in term	u̇	in put	ə	= i in pencil
i	in it	ü	in rule	ə	= o in lemon
ī	in ice	ch	in child	ə	= u in circus
o	in hot	ng	in long		

air (âr) A gas that plants and animals need to live. You cannot see **air.** (page 80)

animal (an′ə məl) A living thing that moves about. A giraffe is an **animal** with a long neck. (page 105)

answer questions (an′sər kwes′chənz) Give responses to questions. You can **answer questions** about what you have read. (page 179)

ask questions (ask kwes′chənz) What you can do to find out something you do not know. You can **ask questions** about what you want to learn before you read. (page 179)

B

balance (bal′ əns) A tool that can compare the weights of objects. The **balance** compares the weights of the ball and the toy bear. (page 14)

blubber (blub′ər) The fat of a whale. **Blubber** keeps a whale warm in the ocean. (page 113)

C

classify (klas′ə fi) To put things that are alike in groups. You can **classify** animals by where they live. (page 100)

claws (klôwz) The sharp, curved nails of some animals. The bear uses its **claws** to climb trees. (page 108)

collect data (kə lekt′ dā′tə) To gather information. You **collect data** when you record your observations in pictures or writing. (page 120)

communicate (ke myü′nə kāt) To use words or pictures to share information. You **communicate** when you tell what you did first, next, and last. (page 36)

container (kən tā′ nər) An object that holds things inside it. A liquid takes the shape of its **container.** (page 16)

context clues (kon′tekst klüz) Pictures or words that help you understand what you are reading. The picture can give you **context clues** about how blocks are different. (page 7)

cool (kül) To lower the temperature of something. **Cooling** changes melted wax into solid crayons. (page 41)

D

desert (dez′ ərt) An environment that is very dry. Many plants and animals live in a **desert.** (page 114)

dissolve (di zolv′) Spread throughout a liquid. Salt **dissolves** when it is mixed with water. (page 45)

environment (en vī′ rən mənt) A place where plants and animals live. An **environment** gives plants and animals what they need. (page 103)

estimate (es′tə māt) To make a careful guess about the size or amount of something. You can **estimate** air temperature by how warm or cool it feels. (p. xii)

evaporate (i vap′ə rāt′) Change from a liquid to a gas. Heat from the sunlight causes water to **evaporate.** (page 48)

experiment (ek sper′ə mənt) use scientific methods to test a hypothesis. You can do an **experiment** to find out what happens when air is heated. (page 62)

explore (ek splôr′) To study science in a hands-on manner. You can **explore** the differences between solids, liquids, and gases. (page 6)

fair test (fâr test) To make sure only one thing is changed in an experiment. You plan a **fair test** in an experiment when you choose the one thing that you will change. (page 226)

fall (fôl) The season that comes after summer. **Fall** is cooler than summer. (page 212)

fog (fog) A cloud near the ground. Some summer nights have **fog.** (page 211)

food (füd) Something animals need to live. The bear eats a fish for **food.** (page 87)

food chain (füd chān) The way food passes from one living thing to another. Plants and animals depend on each other through **food chains.** (page 138)

forest (fôr′ist) An environment that has many trees and other plants. Many animals live in a **forest.** (page 106)

freeze (frēz) Change from a liquid to a solid. Water **freezes** when it gets very cold. (page 46)

fur (fėr) The covering on some animals that is like hair. A sea otter has thick **fur** to keep warm in the ocean. (page 112)

G

gas (gas) Something that takes the shape and size of its container. Air is a **gas.** (page 18)

gills (gilz) A body part a fish uses to get air. The fish has **gills** to breathe in water. (page 111)

H

heat (hēt) To increase the temperature of something. **Heating** changes solid wax into a liquid. (page 40)

hooves (hůvz) The hard parts of the feet of some animals. A sheep has **hooves** to climb on rocks. (page 104)

hypothesis (hī poth′ə sis) A statement of one possible way to solve a problem or answer a question. You make and test a **hypothesis** to do an experiment. (page 62)

infer (in fėr′) To use what you have learned or what you know to make a guess about something. You can **infer** what some animals eat by the shape of their teeth. (page 130)

insect (in′sekt) A small animal that has six legs and a hard covering. Some **insects** eat plants. (page 162)

interpret data (in tėr′prit dā′tə)
To use the information you have collected to solve problems or answer questions. You can **interpret** the **data** you collect to find out what they mean.
(page 121)

investigate (in ves′tə gāt)
To solve a problem or answer a question by following steps. You can **investigate** how much space a liquid takes up.
(page 24)

leaves (lēvz) The parts of a plant that make food for the plant. Green **leaves** use sunlight, air, and water to make food.
(page 84)

light (līt) Something a plant needs to live. Plants may get **light** from the Sun. (page 80)

liquid (lik′wid) Something that takes the shape of its container and has its own amount or size. You can pour a **liquid.** (page 16)

living (liv′ing) Things that are alive, grow, and change. Plants and animals are **living** things. (page 79)

M

marsh (märsh) A wetland environment. Many plants and animals live in a **marsh.** (page 144)

material (mə tir′ē əl) What something is made of or used for. A tissue, a paper towel, and a piece of cloth are different **materials.** (page 32)

measure (mezh′ər) To use a tool to compare the size or amount of something. You can use a thermometer to **measure** the temperature of air. (page 218)

melt (melt) Change from a solid into a liquid. Solid wax **melts** when it is heated. (page 42)

mix (miks) To put two or more things together. **Mixing** blue and yellow paint changes the color to green. (page 42)

model (mod′l) A drawing or object that represents something else. You can use pictures to make a **model** of a food chain. (page 154)

N

nest (nest) A shelter that some animals build. Some birds build **nests** in trees. (page 134)

nutrients (nü′trē əntz) Materials that living things need. Plants can get **nutrients** from the soil. (page 83)

observe (əb zėrv′) To use your senses to find out about an object. You can observe what you see, hear, smell, taste, or touch. (page 6)

ocean (ō′shən) An environment that is a large body of salt water. Many animals and plants live in an ocean. (p. 110)

plant (plant) A living thing that cannot move around on its own. This **plant** grows in a forest. (page 106)

predict (pri dikt′) Tell what you think will happen next. You can **predict** what will happen if plants do not get light. (page 90)

property (prop′ər tē) Something that you can observe with your senses. The size of an object is one of its **properties.** (page 9)

put things in order (pu̇t thingz in ôr′dər) Decide what is first, next, and last. You can **put** the **things** that happen in a science activity **in order.** (page 37)

R

rain gauge (rān gāj) A weather tool to measure the amount of rain. The numbers show how much rain falls into a **rain gauge.** (page 187)

relate prior knowledge (ri lāt′ prī′ər nol′ij) To use what you already know to understand something new. You can **relate** your **prior knowledge** about animals to what you are learning now. (page 77)

retell (rē tel′) To tell what you learned in your own words. You can **retell** the main idea of a story. (page 205)

root (rüt) Part of a plant that holds the plant in the ground. **Roots** take in water and nutrients from the soil. (page 83)

S

season (sē′zn) A time of year. Spring, summer, fall, and winter are the four **seasons.** (page 207)

shape (shāp) the way something looks. The ball has a circle **shape.** (page 10)

shelter (shel′tər) A safe place for animals to live. Some animals build nests for **shelter.** (page 134)

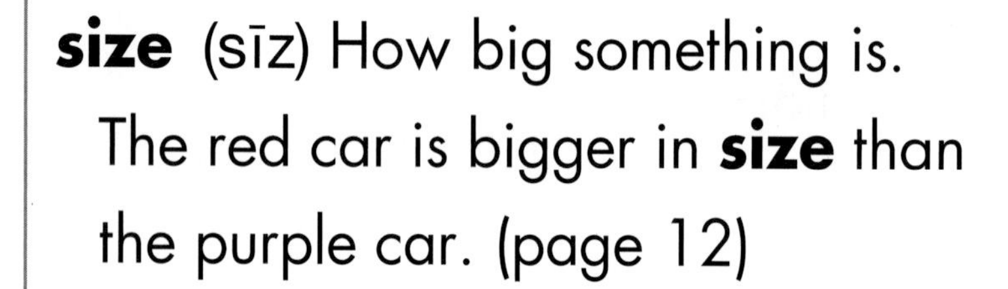

size (sīz) How big something is. The red car is bigger in **size** than the purple car. (page 12)

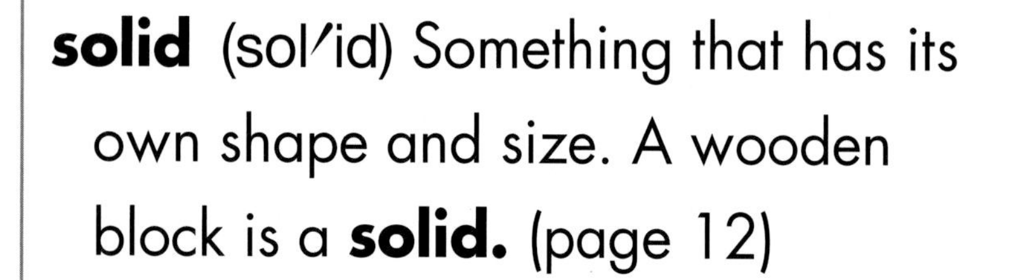

solid (sol′id) Something that has its own shape and size. A wooden block is a **solid.** (page 12)

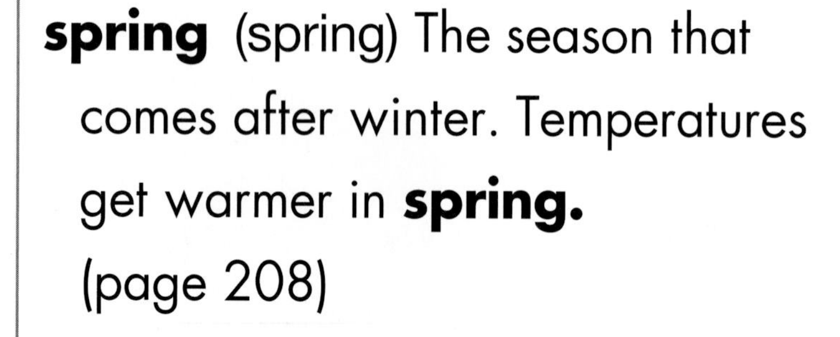

spring (spring) The season that comes after winter. Temperatures get warmer in **spring.** (page 208)

summer (sum′ər) The season that comes after spring. **Summer** may be very dry. (page 210)

Sun (sun) A big ball of hot gas that shines light on Earth. Light from the **Sun** warms the land, water, and air. (page 189)

temperature (tem′per ə chər) How hot or cold something is. You can measure the **temperature** of air. (page 184)

thermometer (thər mom′ ə tər) A tool that measures temperature. The numbers on a **thermometer** show the temperature. (page 185)

water (wô′tər) Liquid that plants, and animals need to live. The bear is drinking **water.** (page 87)

weather (weŦH′ ər) What it is like outside. **Weather** changes from day to day. (page 181)

weight (wāt) How heavy something is. A balance can compare the **weights** of objects (page 14).

wind (wind) Moving air. The **wind** is blowing hard. (page 182)

wind vane (wind vān) A weather tool that tells which way the wind is blowing. A **wind vane** points into the wind. (page 183)

winter (win′tər) The season that comes after fall. **Winter** is the coldest season. (page 214)

Index

This index lists the pages on which topics appear in this book. Page number after a *p* refer to a photograph or drawing.

T

Illustrations

29, 59, 68-69, 95, 125, 159, 197, 223, 231 Kathie Kelleher; 46 Big Sesh Studios; 88 Alan Barnard; 188, 197 Henk Dawson

Photographs

Every effort has been made to secure permission and provide appropriate credit for photographic material. The publisher deeply regrets any omission and pledges to correct errors called to its attention in subsequent editions.

Unless otherwise acknowledged, all photographs are the property of Scott Foresman, a division of Pearson Education.

Photo locators denoted as follows: Top (T), Center (C), Bottom (B), Left (L), Right (R), Background (Bkgd).

Cover: (T) ©Danny Lehman/Corbis, (C) Getty Images

Front Matter: vii (T) Dave King/©DK Images, (B) Martin Cameron/©DK Images; viii (T) ©Craig Tuttle/Corbis, (B) ©Tom Bean/Corbis; ix Corbis; x David Mager, xi ©Royalty-Free/Corbis; xii ©Douglas Faulkner/Photo Researchers, Inc.; xiv ©William Harrigan/Lonely Planet Images; xviii Getty Images

Unit A – Opener: 1 ©Charles Gupton/Corbis; 2 (Bkgd) ©LWA-JDC/Corbis, (B) ©Georgia Kokolis/Getty Images; 3 Getty Images; 4 ©Adrian Myers/Getty Images; 7 ©Adrian Myers/Getty Images; 8 ©Adrian Myers/Getty Images; 12 ©DK Images; 13 ©DK Images; 26 (Bkgd) ©Royalty-Free/Corbis, (TL) ©Adrian Myers/Getty Images, (TCL) ©DK Images; 28 ©DK Images; 30 (BL, Bkgd) NASA; 32 (TL) Corbis, (BR) ©ESA/PLI/Corbis, (Bkgd) ©Photographer's Choice/Getty Images, (B) ©JPL/Cornell/NASA, (CL) NASA, (BR) ©NASA/Corbis; 33 ©Taxi/Getty Images; 37 ©Boden/Ledingham/Masterfile Corporation; 38 ©Boden/Ledingham/Masterfile Corporation; 39 Andy Crawford/©DK Images; 40 (TL) Getty Images, (Bkgd) ©Gale Zucker; 41 ©Gale Zucker; 44 Getty Images; 50 (BR) Martin Cameron/©DK Images, (TL) ©Rita Maas/Getty Images, (BL) Dave King/©DK Images; 51 ©photolibrary/Index Open; 56 (Bkgd) ©Gordon Wiltsie/Getty Images, (TL) ©Boden/Ledingham/Masterfile Corporation, (CL) ©Royalty-Free/Corbis, (BL) Martin Cameron/©DK Images; 60 Courtesy David Smith Photography, (Bkgd) Getty Images, (TR) ©James L. Amos/Corbis; 61 (B) ©Georgia Kokolis/Getty Images, (TL) Getty Images, (T) ©LWA- JDC/Corbis, (CL) ©Taxi/Getty Images; 65 Digital Vision; 66 Getty Images; **Unit B – Opener:** 71 (Bkgd) ©George D. Lepp/Corbis, (TL) ©Martin Ruegner/Getty Images; 72 ©Anthony Arendt/Ambient Images, Inc.; 73 (B) ©Bill Curtsinger/Getty Images, (Bkgd) ©Frans Lanting/Minden Pictures; 74 ©Runk/Schoenberger/Grant Heilman Photography; 75 ©Paul Nicklen/National Geographic Image Collection; 76 ©DK Images; 77 (TR) ©DK Images, (CL) Digital Vision, (Bkgd) ©Paul Nicklen/National Geographic Image Collection; 78 ©Paul Nicklen/National Geographic Image Collection; 79 ©DK Images; 80 (BL) ©Craig Tuttle/Corbis, (TL) Neil Fletcher and Matthew Ward/©DK Images; 81 Getty Images; 82 (TR) ©Runk/Schoenberger/Grant Heilman Photography, (BC, BR, BL) Matthew Ward/©DK Images; 86 ©Royalty-Free/Corbis; 87 ©Tom Brakefield/Corbis; 88 (TL) ©Paul Chesley/Getty Images, (Bkgd) ©Cindy Kassab/Corbis; 92 (Inset) ©Inga Spence/Getty Images, (TL) ©Paul Nicklen/National Geographic Image Collection, (TL) ©Runk/Schoenberger/Grant Heilman Photography, (CL) ©Tom Brakefield/Corbis; 95 Matthew Ward/©DK Images; 96 (Bkgd) ©John Elk III/Getty Images, (TR) ©ZSSD/Minden Pictures, (BL) ©Konrad Wothe/Minden Pictures; 97 ©Norbert Wu/Minden Pictures; 98 ©W. Perry Conway/Corbis; 99 ©Zig Leszczynski/Animals Animals/Earth Scenes; 100 ©Tom & Pat Leeson/Photo Researchers, Inc.; 101 (CR, BL) Getty Images; 102 ©W. Perry Conway/Corbis; 103 (TR) ©Jeremy Thomas/Natural Visions, (BR) ©Taxi/Getty Images; 104 (TL, CL, BL) ©DK Images, (Bkgd) ©Kevin Schafer/Corbis; 105 ©Art Wolfe/Getty Images; 106 (BL) Peter Chadwick/©DK Images, (TL) ©Theo Allofs/zefa/Corbis, (Bkgd) ©John Warden/Getty Images; 108 (TL, BL) ©David Welling/Animals Animals/Earth Scenes, (R) ©Tom Brakefield/Corbis; 109 ©John D. Cunningham/Visuals Unlimited; 110 (TL) ©Stone/Getty Images, (R) Digital Vision, (BR) ©Randy Morse/Animals Animals/Earth Scenes, (BL) ©Flip Nicklin/Minden Pictures, (BL) ©Ralph A. Clevenger/Corbis; 111 Getty Images; 112 (TL) ©Randy Morse/Animals Animals/Earth Scenes, (B) ©Lightwave Photography, Inc./Animals Animals/Earth Scenes; 113 (TR) ©Bill Coster/NHPA Limited, (Bkgd) ©Bob Cranston/Seapics; 114 (TL) ©Zig Leszczynski/Animals Animals/Earth Scenes, (BR) ©Karl Switak/NHPA Limited; 115 (Bkgd) ©Tom Bean/Corbis, (TL) ©Doug Sokell/Visuals Unlimited; 116 (TL) ©Gerlach Nature Photography/Animals Animals/Earth Scenes, (Bkgd) ©Daniel Heuclin/NHPA Limited; 117 (TL) ©David Kjaer/Nature Picture Library, (TR) ©Gerlach Nature Photography/Animals Animals/Earth Scenes; 118 (T) ©Nigel J. Dennis/NHPA Limited, (B) ©Art Wolfe/Stone/Getty Images; 122 (Bkgd) ©Frans Lanting/Corbis, (TL) ©W. Perry Conway/Corbis, (TL) ©Tom Brakefield/Corbis, (CL) ©Flip Nicklin/Minden Pictures, (BL) ©Daniel Heuclin/NHPA Limited, (BR) ©Kevin Schafer/Corbis; 124 (BCL) ©Tom Brakefield/Corbis, (BCR) ©John D. Cunningham/Visuals Unlimited, (TR) Digital Vision, (BR) Getty Images, (BL) ©Bob Cranston/Seapics, (T) ©Tom Bean/Corbis; 125 ©Karl Switak/NHPA Limited; 126 (T) ©Alan Schroeder/Courtesy of Sonia Ortega, (B) ©John Bova/Photo Researchers, Inc.; 127 ©Michael S. Quinton/Getty Images; 128 (T) Corbis, (BL) ©David Weintraub/Stock Boston, (BR) ©Mark Moffet/Minden Pictures, (BC) ©Karl Switak/NHPA Limited; 129 (BR) ©Galen Rowell/Corbis, (BC) ©John Cancalosi/Nature Picture Library, (BL) ©Nature's Images/Photo Researchers, Inc.; 131 (Bkgd) ©Joseph Sohm/ChromoSohm Inc./Corbis, (C) ©The Image Bank/Getty Images; 132 ©Joseph Sohm/ChromoSohm Inc./Corbis; 133 (TL) ©DK Images, (BR) ©Kennan Ward/Corbis; 134 (TL) Corbis, (BR) ©Kenneth M. Highfill/Photo Researchers, Inc., (CL) ©Alan G. Nelson/Animals Animals/Earth Scenes, (BC) ©Stephen Dalton/NHPA Limited; 135 (BR) Corbis, (TR) ©NHMPL/Getty Images; 136 (TL) ©James L. Amos/Photo Researchers, Inc., (B) ©Bill Banaszewski/Visuals Unlimited; 137 (TR) ©James L. Amos/Photo Researchers, Inc., (TL)

©Alan Williams/NHPA Limited, (BR) ©Ron Sanford/Corbis; 138 (TL) ©Peter Lilja/Getty Images, (BL) ©DK Images; 139 ©George D. Lepp/Corbis; 140 (BR) ©Mark Moffet/Minden Pictures, (BL) ©Karl Switak/NHPA Limited; 141 ©Nature's Images/Photo Researchers, Inc.; 142 (BL) ©Nature's Images/Photo Researchers, Inc., (TL, BR) ©John Cancalosi/ Nature Picture Library, (CR) ©Galen Rowell/Corbis; 143 (BCR) ©Mark Moffet/Minden Pictures, (BR) ©Karl Switak/ NHPA Limited, (TCR) ©John Cancalosi/Nature Picture Library, (TR) ©Galen Rowell/Corbis; 144 (TL, CR) ©Robert Erwin/NHPA Limited, (BL) ©David Weintraub/Stock Boston, (CR) Dr. D. A. Gray/University of California-Northridge; 145 ©Dan Suzio/Photo Researchers, Inc.; 146 (BL) ©Dan Suzio/ Photo Researchers, Inc., (C) ©Joe MacDonald/Corbis; 147 (TCR) ©Joe MacDonald/Corbis, (CR) ©Dan Suzio/Photo Researchers, Inc., (BR) ©David Weintraub/Stock Boston, (BCR) ©Robert Erwin/NHPA Limited, (BR) Dr. D. A. Gray/ University of California-Northridge; 148 (TL, CL) Philip Dowell/©DK Images, (Bkgd) ©Martin Harvey/Peter Arnold, Inc.; 149 Digital Vision; 150 (TL) ©Grant Heilman Photography, (Bkgd) ©Lester Lefkowitz/Getty Images; 151 ©Grant Heilman Photography; 152 ©John Shaw/Tom Stack & Associates, Inc.; 153 (CL) ©John Gerlach/Visuals Unlimited, (TC) ©Tim Wright/Corbis, (C) ©William J. Weber/Visuals Unlimited, (CCR) ©Taxi/Getty Images, (TR) ©Michael Sewell/Peter Arnold, Inc., (BL) ©DK Images, (TL) ©Michael & Patricia Fogden/Corbis; 156 (Bkgd) ©Harvey Lloyd/Getty Images, (TL) ©Joseph Sohm/ChromoSohm Inc./ Corbis, (TCL) ©Bill Banaszewski/Visuals Unlimited, (CL) ©DK Images, (BCL) ©Galen Rowell/Corbis, (BL) ©David Weintraub/Stock Boston, (BL) Digital Vision, (BR) ©George D. Lepp/Corbis; 158 (CL, TR) ©David Weintraub/Stock Boston, (CR) ©Joe MacDonald/Corbis, (BR) ©Grant Heilman Photography, (TR) ©Dan Suzio/Photo Researchers, Inc., (TR) ©Robert Erwin/NHPA Limited, (CL) Corbis, (TR) Dr. D. A. Gray/University of California-Northridge; 160 (B) ©Marian Bacon/Animals Animals/Earth Scenes, (B) Getty Images, (Bkgd) Map Resources; 161 (TR) ©Andrew Syred/Photo Researchers, Inc., (T) ©Royalty-Free/Corbis, (BR) MFSC/ NASA; 162 (BL) ©Kate Bennett Mendz/Animals Animals/ Earth Scenes, (TR, TC, TR, BC) Jerry Young/©DK Images, (BR, CR) ©Royalty-Free/Corbis, (CL, BR) ©DK Images; 163 (CL) ©Norbert Wu/Minden Pictures, (CL) ©Michael S. Quinton/ Getty Images, (B) ©Anthony Arendt/Ambient Images, Inc., (TL) ©Frans Lanting/Minden Pictures; 164 ©Ian Beames/ Ecoscene/Corbis; 166 ©Mark Fallander/OnAsia; 167 Getty Images; 168 ©Stockbyte/Getty Images; **Unit C – Opener:** 173 ©Ron and Patty Thomas/Getty Images; 174 ©Morton Beebe/Corbis; 175 ©Richard Kaylin/Getty Images; 176 (BL) Dave King/©DK Images, (BR) ©Nigel J. Dennis/Gallo Images/Corbis, (Bkgd) Getty Images, (TC) ©Ariel Skelley/ Masterfile Corporation; 177 (TL) ©Bruce Peebles/Corbis, (BL) ©Taxi/Getty Images; 179 ©Ariel Skelley/Masterfile Corporation; 180 (Bkgd) Getty Images, (Bkgd) ©Ariel Skelley/Masterfile Corporation; 181 David Mager; 182 (TL) Dave King/©DK Images, (B) ©Taxi/Getty Images; 183 Dave King/©DK Images; 184 ©Stephen Beaudet/Corbis; 185 (CL) ©Nigel J. Dennis/Gallo Images/Corbis, (CR) ©Marc Muench/Corbis; 186 (TL) Hemera Technologies, (R) ©Taxi/ Getty Images; 188 (Bkgd) ©Michael McQueen/Getty Images, (CR, CL) Getty Images; 190 (TCL) ©Taxi/Getty Images, (Bkgd) ©The Image Bank/Getty Images; 191 ©Bruce Peebles/Corbis; 192 ©Marc Muench/Corbis; 194 (Bkgd) ©Dennie Cody/Getty Images, (BL) ©Michael McQueen/Getty Images, (TL) ©Ariel Skelley/Masterfile Corporation, (BR) Dave King/©DK Images; 196 (TR) Getty Images, (TR) ©Taxi/Getty Images; 198 (BR) ©Jacques Descloitres/MODIS Rapid Response Team/GSFC/NASA, (Bkgd) ©Royalty-Free/Corbis, (TR) Getty Images, (BL) ©Reuters/Corbis; 200 (TL) ©John Mead/Photo Researchers, Inc., (BL, BR) ©Goddard Space Flight Center/NASA; 201 ©Wes Walker/Getty Images; 202 (BL, B) ©Royalty-Free/ Corbis, (BR) ©Morton Beebe/Corbis; 203 ©Timothy Laman/ National Geographic Image Collection; 205 (Bkgd) ©Marc Muench/Corbis, (CR) ©Tim Barnett/Getty Images; 206 ©Marc Muench/Corbis; 207 ©Klaus Hackenberg/Zefa/ Corbis; 208 (B) ©Royalty-Free/Corbis, (TL) ©Roy Morsch/ Corbis; 209 ©Patricio Robles Gil/Nature Picture Library; 210 (TL) Hemera Technologies, (Bkgd) ©Royalty-Free/Corbis; 211 ©Garry Blac/Masterfile Corporation; 212 (TL, C, BL) Hemera Technologies, (BR) Peter Anderson/©DK Images, (C) Panoramic Images; 213 ©Morton Beebe/Corbis; 214 (TL) Hemera Technologies, (C) ©Tony Freeman/PhotoEdit, (Bkgd) ©Timothy Laman/National Geographic Image Collection; 215 ©George D. Lepp/Corbis; 216 (Bkgd) ©Gabe Palmer/ Corbis, (C) ©Stone/Getty Images; 217 (TL) Getty Images, (TL) Hemera Technologies; 218 ©Royalty-Free/Corbis; 220 (Bkgd) Getty Images, (TL) ©Marc Muench/Corbis, (CL) ©Royalty-Free/Corbis, (CL) Panoramic Images, (BL) ©Tony Freeman/PhotoEdit, (B) Peter Anderson/©DK Images; 222 (CL, TL) ©Royalty-Free/Corbis, (TC) ©Morton Beebe/Corbis, (TR) ©Marc Muench/Corbis; 224 (Bkgd) ©Bruce Wilson/ Getty Images, (BR) ©Adrian Weinbrecht/Getty Images; 225 (B) ©Morton Beebe/Corbis, (TL) ©Richard Kaylin/Getty Images, (CL) ©Wes Walker/Getty Images; 226 Getty Images; 229 Getty Images; 230 (B) ©David Young-Wolff/ PhotoEdit, (Bkgd) ©Wides & Holl/Getty Images

End Matter: EM5 ©Art Wolfe/Getty Images; EM7 ©Tom Brakefield/Corbis; EM8 ©Tom Bean/Corbis; EM10 (B) ©Flip Nicklin/Minden Pictures, (T) ©Morton Beebe/Corbis; EM11 (T) ©Garry Blac/Masterfile Corporation, (TCR) ©Royalty-Free/Corbis, (B) ©Lightwave Photography, Inc./Animals Animals/Earth Scenes, (BCC) ©John Warden/Getty Images, (CR) ©David Kjaer/Nature Picture Library, (CR) ©Karl Switak/NHPA Limited, (CR) ©Mark Moffet/Minden Pictures, (CR) ©Galen Rowell/Corbis, (CR) ©Nature's Images/Photo Researchers, Inc., (TC) ©Norbert Wu/Minden Pictures; EM12 (BC) ©Gale Zucker, (B) ©Kevin Schafer/Corbis; EM13 Jerry Young/©DK Images; EM14 Getty Images; EM15 (C) ©Paul Nicklen/National Geographic Image Collection, (B) ©David Weintraub/Stock Boston, (B) ©Royalty-Free/Corbis; EM16 ©Alan G. Nelson/Animals Animals/Earth Scenes; EM17 Digital Vision; EM18 ©Adrian Myers/Getty Images; EM20 (T) ©Kennan Ward/Corbis, (C, B) ©Royalty-Free/Corbis; EM21 (B) ©Ariel Skelley/Masterfile Corporation, (BC) ©Tom Brakefield/Corbis, (T) ©Marc Muench/Corbis; EM22 (C) Dave King/©DK Images, (T) ©Taxi/Getty Images, (B) ©Tony Freeman/PhotoEdit

End Sheets: (R) ©GK & Vikki Hart/Getty Images, (Bkgd) ©Chris Cheadle/Getty Images